ANIMAL
LESSONS

About the Author

Danielle MacKinnon (Boston, MA) is a highly gifted intuitive and coach who has appeared on TV and radio around the world. She's also an esteemed faculty member at the Omega Institute, the Kripalu Center, and many other globally recognized teaching and wellness institutions. Her school, the Danielle MacKinnon School of Animal Communication, has given the field of animal communication more global visibility than ever before. Each year Danielle leads thousands of people through their challenges and into a world of miraculous possibility. Visit her online at www.DanielleMacKinnon.com.

ANIMAL LESSONS

Discovering Your
Spiritual Connection with Animals

DANIELLE MACKINNON

Llewellyn Publications
Woodbury, Minnesota

First Edition
First Printing, 2017

Cover photo: Getty Images 127543971, OPIFICIO 42
Cover design: Lisa Novak

Llewellyn Publications is a registered trademark of Llewellyn Worldwide Ltd.

Library of Congress Cataloging-in-Publication Data (Pending)
ISBN: 978-0-7387-5135-1

Llewellyn Worldwide Ltd. does not participate in, endorse, or have any authority or responsibility concerning private business transactions between our authors and the public.

All mail addressed to the author is forwarded but the publisher cannot, unless specifically instructed by the author, give out an address or phone number.

Any Internet references contained in this work are current at publication time, but the publisher cannot guarantee that a specific location will continue to be maintained. Please refer to the publisher's website for links to authors' websites and other sources.

Llewellyn Publications
A Division of Llewellyn Worldwide Ltd.
2143 Wooddale Drive
Woodbury, MN 55125-2989
www.llewellyn.com

Printed in the United States of America

Also by Danielle MacKinnon

Soul Contracts: Find Harmony and Unlock Your Brilliance

Featured In

Llewellyn's Complete Book of Mindful Living·

Acknowledgments

"An animal heart does not have the same boundaries or conditions as the human heart. It is more tolerant, more transparent. The human is to learn to remove the limits on her heart. The animal is to show her how."

—Amy Weiss

I could not have written this book without the unconditional love of each and every animal I've ever known.

In gratitude...

Dedicated to Kev

Contents

INTRODUCTION

You may have picked up this book because you're a huge animal lover and thought it sounded pretty cool when you read that it's possible to work with your pet to create a better you. Or perhaps you are at your wit's end dealing with a pet's behavior problem and are willing to try anything—and this book represents that. You may be thinking, however, that the concept of helping an animal by helping yourself does seem a little crazy. Well, I completely understand this (and would have thought the same thing myself had I not witnessed it working with thousands of people over the past decade and a half).

Many books have been written about the love of a good pet, but none have yet shown how that love (inherent to *all* animals) fulfills a greater purpose: specifically helping people evolve into the best possible humans they can be while at the same time helping animals live better lives, become better behaved, and experience better treatment. Countless books have tackled "curing" behavior problems and mastering animal training, but none have demonstrated how working on yourself is actually the key to a positive, healthy, problem-free relationship with an animal in your life. To fix "problems," most books focus on animal training, which means they miss the main point: if we pay attention, our pets (and other animals, whether wild, farm, or domesticated) can catalyze our emotional, spiritual, and mental growth—all of which result in better jobs, more love, better loves, kinder friends, more fun, happier days, and, not to mention, behavior challenges fading away!

Animals are already creating tremendous shifts in people in mainstream society. Animal Planet, for example, features a reality TV program called *Pit Bulls & Parolees* about an animal rescue center that hires parolees and works with a very misunderstood breed of dog: pit bulls. Through the act of rehabilitating and caring for abused and forgotten dogs, the inmates learn responsibility, respect, self-care, and more. Programs like this are so successful at helping inmates become happier, healthier people that there are many of them taking place in prisons around the country, and this isn't even the tip of the iceberg!

Additionally, equine-assisted therapy programs that use horses as a system of treatment for children with autism have become very popular around the world. This is a form of care that uses the rhythmic movement of riding a horse to help children focus better through their body. Then, the healing is pushed even further ahead as the children learn how to take care of the horse. Autistic children in these types of programs typically become more communicative, calmer, and even happier.

The *Pit Bulls & Parolees* TV show, equine-assisted therapy programs, and numerous other programs have achieved great successes, and much of the world is embracing methods such as these. But what if it were possible to take these ideas even further? What if animals could understand what you need, what you want to express, and what will help you move through a troubling period, and then through this understanding, they could even assist you in changing your beliefs?

What if your pet could actually play the role of your therapist?

We are all familiar with the idea that animals are extra sensitive to their surroundings. Housecats know when their humans are sad, dogs sense when excitement is in the air, wild birds know when danger is approaching, and elephants are aware of the near or far location of their entire family. But have you considered that animals might be even more in tune with their surroundings than previously thought?

Animal Lessons

The animals in your life are so very connected to you and to their environment that they understand if you don't feel safe in the world, if deep down you don't like yourself very much, or if you don't feel worthy of a loving, caring, nurturing relationship. Animals can understand these things about you better than, perhaps, you currently understand yourself. Because of all this knowledge animals have about us humans, animals are then able to modify their behavior (positively or negatively) in order to force us to address these deep-down, negative feelings about ourselves, thereby improving the quality of our lives more than we ever thought possible before.

Through my work with animals as an animal intuitive, I've learned that animals are acting as our therapists, our trainers, our mentors, and our teachers, guiding (and sometimes pushing) us to take leaps in order to move to the next step in our own evolution. Want to stand up to your tyrant mother? Look to your aggressive dog. Want to find love? Pay attention to the anxious squirrel in your backyard. Is your job sucking the life out of you? Check out what your sick horse is showing you. Yes, it may sound crazy, but our animals are giving us the answers—every single day.

Incredibly, this phenomenon isn't just for people who have "exceptional" animals. It occurs with all animals, from mice to camels to dogs to elephants to any animal you can name. Isn't it exciting to think about finding a way to tap into the wisdom, intuition, and growth that animals have been offering humans for thousands of years?

Although I'm an animal communicator, this is not an intuitive animal communication book. Not at all. It is a book about what the animals are communicating to us through their behaviors and through the feelings and emotions they evoke in us. For more than fifteen years I've been working as a professional animal communicator, and during that time I've encountered thousands of people and their pets and wild animals. I've come to understand that there is a lot more to the human-animal relationship than most people (even the biggest animal lovers!) have realized.

In my business as an animal communicator, people bring their animals to see me because they want me to use my intuitive abilities to fix a problem. Perhaps their dog was peeing in inappropriate places, their horse was afraid of his stall in the barn, the mother hen in their coop has been pulling her feathers out, or the mountain lion who lives across the way is killing all the chickens. My clients will tear up while explaining their hope that I will be able to talk the animal into behaving differently or, more appropriately, that I'll be able to bring their challenge to an immediate resolution. And at first, when I began doing this intuitive work with animals, this is what I thought I was supposed to do too—fix everyone and get rid of the behavior problems. Make everything for the person and their animal nice and easy.

It turned out that sentiment couldn't have been more wrong. At least, I was completely wrong about how "fixing" the animals would happen—it wasn't the animals that needed the fixing!

No animal wanted me to say, "Hey! There's nothing scary in the barn. You have to start walking in there without freaking out!" Just like no human would want to be told, "Elevators aren't terrifying, get over it!" This "explain it and fix it" approach wasn't changing the behavior of the animals my clients were bringing to me, and because of that, it certainly wasn't making my clients happy either.

As I delved more deeply into this work, though, I found that there was a thread—one very important thread. The animals (and it didn't matter if they were pets, farm animals, wild animals, or any other kind) that people were bringing to me to fix seemed to have a much better understanding of themselves and their behavior than their humans (and, at first, I) ever suspected, and they were very aware of the challenges and waves they were creating for their humans.

Animals have been secretly helping people evolve for thousands of years, but people have not given this assistance the credit it deserves. I want to show you what I've learned through my many years working deeply and intuitively with animals so that you can take full advantage of all that the animal kingdom has to offer at every level. You'll learn:

- How your own pet is helping you grow and evolve
- What life lesson your pet is assisting you in mastering
- How to "fix" that behavior problem in a beloved animal (oh, those behavior problems!)

- What your life can look like once you've mastered what your animal is teaching you
- How your animal is helping you be more confident, feel better about yourself, and feel comfortable being seen
- How your animal can shift your life so you can create more abundance
- How to accept the love that all animals (and people) hold for you
- Fun, goofy tools and techniques to help keep you on track
- Specific, easy-to-follow steps for mastering the lesson from your pet so you can evolve and grow!

I always say this to my clients, so I will say it here too: this is not hard work. Once you know what to look out for and what steps to take, the only challenging part is making yourself do it. If you're an animal lover like most people I know, you'll jump at the chance to work deeply with the animal in your life, especially when you learn that the work you do on yourself will benefit both of you as well as the other areas of your life!

This work with animals isn't something you master and then move on from. It is an ongoing exploration of yourself, your life, and your inner beauty. In my personal life, I've had opportunity after opportunity to witness animals in this way, and it hasn't mattered how much I've learned from each experience or how much I've progressed as a result of that learning: the animals continue to find new ways to teach and enlighten me.

How to Use This Book

People are surprised, at the beginning of one of my classes, when one of the first things I say is that "the animal in your life wants to help you become a better person." I know it sounds crazy—how could an animal actually want that? And it's not usually what people who are struggling with a pet's behavior problem, feeling bad for an animal in the wild, or raising a hundred chickens on their farm are used to thinking about. But my experience as an animal communicator has shown me something different about animals than most people realize, and it's through this book that I want to share what I've learned through thousands upon thousands of hours working with people and animals over the past almost twenty years. It's my experience, and it's the experience of the animals and the humans I've come into contact with. And it's been life-changing for them as well as for me. This book provides the missing link between what you see going on around you in how animals are treated globally and what you are feeling in your heart.

In this book, I'm going to help you understand why your dog is acting crazy, why your chickens (and only *your* chickens) choose to behave the way they do, and why your heart breaks for the plight of a wild animal you've only heard about. Then you're going to learn how to harness that understanding, so you can walk away empowered from within, feeling better about yourself and having a deeper, more positive relationship with the animals you encounter in your life.

It's a book that could be called a self-help book, because you will get a lot of information that assists you in understanding your-self better, but it's also an animal training book, because as you work through the book and begin employing the tools and tech-niques, your relationships with the animals that come into your life will change greatly and for the better. Your dog can stop barking. The cows can stop escaping. The cat's health can improve.

Yes, it's a self-help book. Yes, it's an animal training book, but—and I hope I don't sound too biased here—it's also a book that will connect you to the world of animals in the way that I believe we're all meant to be connected.

Animals have mastered the unconditional love of themselves and of the world they live in. The human race has so much to learn from them, and in my animal communication work I continue to learn every day, despite the huge number of animals I've already worked with. I resisted this work for a long time, but when it had a profound soul-reaching effect on my well-being and on who I viewed myself to be, I had to stand up, take notice, and start sharing this realization with others.

Read on with an open heart and an open mind, full of trust. Everything I talk about here in *Animal Lessons* stems directly from my experiences with animals. It's what they have shown me again and again, and it's what they want you to know!

My Personal Experience

I resisted this understanding about animals for a long time and only finally embraced it when I felt I had no other choice (and boy, am I glad I finally did!). For almost twenty years, I've been working intuitively with animals and their humans, but that path wasn't always clear to me or even desired.

I graduated from the University of New Hampshire with a bachelor's degree in English and within a year found myself living in the heart of the Mission in San Francisco. My husband and I had known each other through college, but it wasn't until I moved to California that we started dating, and within three months we were engaged. I was so happy, as I'd finally met someone who understood my sensitivity! He didn't make fun of me for saving bugs trapped in the house or for helping dogs that looked like strays. In fact, despite being somewhat of a manly man (quiet and protective), he joined right in and began saving animals himself. It was such a relief to finally have someone in my life who didn't view my sensitivity as a weakness or a drawback or something that I needed to change.

I grew up in the Midwest, feeling as if I stood out like a sore thumb. I'm tall and skinny (no matter how much I work out), and while that may seem like it would be a blessing, for me it was a curse. None of my friends had the same body type, and as a teenage girl, not fitting in was unacceptable. Top that off with the fact that I seemed to know what everyone around me was thinking or feeling—without being told—and you can begin to see that I spent almost the first twenty years of my life feeling like a misfit.

After a couple years in San Francisco with Kevin, we both decided it was time to go to grad school. Kevin's dream was to get his master's in geology, while my dream was to be in charge. I went for my MBA. At the time, all I knew was that I wanted my own business. My focus wasn't on helping people or animals but more on finding something to do with myself that made me happy. I thought getting an MBA and moving into the corporate world would do that.

It didn't. While I excelled in the corporate world (I do love structure!), I didn't find that it was feeding my soul. I also found that my straightforward way of dealing with problems and challenges wasn't the norm, and once again I felt like a misfit.

Around that time, our dog Bella became gravely ill. Kevin and I checked her into our vet, and over a period of four days she continued to go downhill with an unknown sickness. As each day came and went, I found myself less and less able to go to work and deal with the politics, projects, and dysfunctions that were there, and it felt much better to work out my frustrations and fear at the gym. And that's when it happened.

I ran into my friend Cindy in the gym parking lot. Cindy and I had originally met because she had a dog-walking business. She knew both of my dogs Bella and Kelso very well and loved them as much as I did. She said, "Danielle, since you're out of options, I have an idea. Why don't you take her to see this pet psychic I heard about? He's up in Nashua this weekend."

Now, I'd grown up doing everything I could to blend in to my Midwest and, later in my teenage years, New England environment, which meant not delving deeply into things like psychics, energy healing, near-death experiences, or pet psychics. But as a married adult woman working a job in the corporate world, I finally felt secure enough in myself to run (not walk) home, call the pet psychic, and immediately make an appointment for the next day.

I was not only excited to possibly help my dog, I was also excited to possibly have it proven to me that animals really were able to communicate in this way.

The pet psychic reading on Bella proved to be not only true but also a success. As a result, Bella did get better and went on to live to be fourteen years old despite being a puppy mill dog rescued from a terrible pet shop. I call it a success because it was during the reading that I realized two things: First, this stuff is real. This guy was really, actually, truly, communicating through ESP or something with my dogs. And second, not only could I do this, but I have been doing it my entire life.

Although I opened up my own pet psychic business within just a few months, I hemmed and hawed over leaving the corporate world (and my corporate salary) for a few years. It wasn't until I was laid off from my job as a project manager at a major telecom company that I finally took the leap and said, "Okay, this is it. I'm doing it, and I'm doing it full time!"

At that same time, I was also dealing with feelings of being an outsider. My family could not understand how I would want to consider leaving a very promising career in marketing at a very successful company to go and pursue my love of animals in this way. Most likely, if I'd received their support, I would have jumped sooner into working full time as an animal communicator, but had I done that, I'm not sure I'd be where I am today.

During that time, one of the things I was experiencing was that I didn't seem to have control over the readings. In my eyes an animal communicator connects psychically with an animal, asks the animal some questions, delivers the answers to the animal's human, and fixes whatever the problem was. If I was going to do this animal communication thing, then I wanted to do it right. And I wanted to look to how other animal communicators were working and follow their examples.

But that wasn't the plan the animals had for me. And as I would soon find out, "fitting in" and "following the crowd" were not in my future.

How I Reluctantly Discovered Animal Lessons

As I connected intuitively to each animal, the animal would tell me I should also be connecting to his or her human. Right away, this was not what I wanted to do. It wasn't the norm of what I saw other animal communicators do, and it felt like I was psychically prying into the life of the person. But the animals wouldn't talk with me unless I did it their way! So my work began involving animals and any people connected to them.

Next, when I worked with my clients' pets, they weren't content to just have me connect to their people. They wanted me to intuitively get to know their personalities. They showed me how to psychically detect things about that person that I feared the person didn't want me to know.

"Ah, I see you're a real go-getter at work, Mike, but it turns out you really hate your job and would rather be doing something artsy." And I'd have to say this to a guy who just brought his pit bull to me so that I could help him with his chewing problem! Now, imagine having to do that! I couldn't and didn't want to, so I resisted. In my connection to the animal I would say, "Yeah, yeah, okay, but tell me about this chewing thing," and in my head the dog would say something like, "Don't you get it? He's supposed to be painting!" I was so scared to tell the person what I was getting.

This all changed with Jesus the Chihuahua. That little dog had the power to alter the course of my entire life—and he probably only weighed six pounds.

In a phone session, Diane wanted me to work with her dog, Jesus, because he was peeing in a plant in the kitchen, and it was killing the plant. Diane wanted me to fix Jesus so that he'd begin using the backyard, as it was causing a lot of turmoil in the home to have Jesus peeing indoors. To me and my resistant little self, it seemed like an open and shut case. All I needed to do was connect to Jesus, tell him to pee outside using the sliding door, and all would be well.

Ha!

Jesus had quite a lot of spunk. He was no wilting flower and didn't really seem to feel that his small stature put him in any danger. When I connected psychically with him I began right off by asking about the peeing in the plant. I asked if he knew that he wasn't supposed to pee in the plant.

"Yes, Danielle. I know that," he said to me.

I immediately thought it could be a bladder problem and asked him how his bladder was.

"My bladder is fine, Danielle," he said, as if he were talking to a little kid.

It must be a training issue then! I asked if he knew where the backyard was.

"Of course, Danielle. I know where the backyard is—it's right out there," he answered in my head with somewhat of an eye roll.

I asked if he knew how to get outside.

"Yes, Danielle! Clearly, I know how to pee outside!" he almost yelled psychically in my head.

Now, I was at a loss. This wasn't a training issue—he knew what he was doing. I told him then that he should stop peeing in the plant. I told him it was causing problems for his family and that things would calm down if he would just pee where he is supposed to pee.

"No, it won't."

Huh? Diane had told me that he was the cause of the problems in the family, and now he's telling me that he's not the cause. I realized I had never asked him *why* he was peeing in the plant.

I was almost hit over the head with his psychic answer. He showed me an image of a man and a woman in the kitchen fighting. The man was reaching over and punching the woman and the woman was covering her face as the man continued to hit her. I realized there was quite a lot of domestic violence going on in the home, and I suddenly felt at a loss. What was I supposed to do with this information? And how did it have anything to do with Jesus peeing in the plant?

Jesus provided the answer. He psychically told me that he was peeing in the plant during the times when Diane needed to be taking care of herself. Every moment that he peed in the plant was a moment where Diane needed to stop whatever she was doing and reevaluate her choices. He said that as she got better at taking care of herself, he would have less and less need to remind her by peeing in the plant. Dumbfounded, I remember holding the phone to my ear, not knowing what to tell Diane about what Jesus had just told me.

I didn't want to tell Diane I knew about the abuse.

I didn't want to tell Diane that she needed to take better care of herself.

And I certainly didn't want to tell Diane that her dog would only stop peeing in the plant in the kitchen once she'd begun living an empowered life in which she was the number one priority.

Silence. For quite a few seconds. Luckily, most people don't understand how an animal intuitive works, so she didn't have any idea the quiet was due to my own freak-out in my head. Finally, I asked Jesus how I should tell this to Diane. He gracefully told me the wording, which I felt comfortable using, and I immediately shared with Diane what he had said about taking care of herself.

It was this reading that made me finally agree to follow this path that the animals had been carving out for me all along. It was this reading that also made me abandon all hope of ever fitting in with the rest of the world. If I was going to do this animal work thing, then I was going to do it the way the animals were making me do it.

Since that time, the animals have helped me perfect connecting with their person. Whether it's a pet, an animal in a zoo, a wild animal, an animal on a farm, or even an animal discovered through social media, every single animal has held the same basic message. I've appeared on countless radio shows, on TV, on telesummits, at events, at workshops, and at retreats with the same message: animals are here to help us evolve and finally embrace unconditional love. Unconditional love for them—and even more importantly, unconditional love for all, including ourselves.

In my private practice, when someone first comes to me, even if they are the biggest animal lover they know of, there is always another level of love they can discover for themselves through working with animals. One of my favorite times of the summer is when I teach beginning Soul-Level Animal Communication at the Omega Institute in Rhinebeck, New York. We spend three days connecting with beloved pets, teaching our animals and each other's animals, but on the last day of the workshop, I send everyone out into the wilderness to find a wild animal of some kind to connect with and learn from. The first time I taught the class most people connected with the groundhogs or the deer that frequent the Omega campus, but as time has gone on, the students have expanded their experiences. They now connect with beetles, butterflies, hummingbirds, chipmunks, slugs, and more. And because they just spent the past few days coming to understand how animals are helping us evolve, they always come back having learned about themselves through these wild encounters.

This is what I want to share with you—how to benefit from your experiences and relationships with animals you come to know. This, I have realized, is how you can discover unconditional love for all—especially yourself.

Chapter One

THE SYSTEM OF ANIMAL LESSONS

Animal Lessons is a system intended to help you harness that which the animals in your life are teaching you. The system is both practical and fluid, and it can be broken down into a few simple steps that I'll outline for you here. These easy steps will show you how to gain a solid understanding of how animals (whether domesticated, wild, farm, or other) are acting as your mentors, therapists, trainers, and gurus every day. One of the main tenets of this program is developing and holding a new-found awareness of yourself, but this awareness requires solid groundwork from which to grow.

The Five Steps to Animal Lessons

To get you primed, here's a very brief outline of the steps.

Step 1: Determine How Your Animal Is Helping You

The first step is very logical: determine *how* an animal is helping you grow, evolve, change, learn, or become a master. Your pet (or any animal you feel a special connection to) already knows this and is seeing it through, but your experience of this animal probably hasn't made you aware of that yet. Determining how your animal is helping you is one of the most important aspects, as things with our animals aren't always as they seem. I've worked with people who thought their animal was helping them shift in one area of their life, only to delve deeper and discover the learning was actually focused in a different, more profound direction.

Step 2: Determine the Lesson

Once you've figured out how your animal is helping you, the natural question that pops up is *Why?* This is the second step—figuring that out. Why do you need help in this area? What do you need to learn? What belief is this animal helping you change? We'll use my fun technique with your chosen animal (and yes, it may make you feel a little crazy sometimes) to aid you in developing a new kind of awareness of yourself, including identifying what beliefs the animal in your life is helping you change. It's through this awareness that you'll next start identifying how you're avoiding learning this deep lesson. The better your understanding of the belief your animal is helping you change, the more awareness you'll achieve and the easier the process will be. Knowledge is the key here.

Step 3: Find Your Work-Arounds

People seem to have the most fun when they reach step 3 in the process. It takes into account the learning and growth you've now experienced and helps you (with your animal's continued support and assistance) delve more deeply into your awareness, fine-tuning your tools to discover the next layer of this work with your animal. Here you get to discover those automated behavior patterns that are covering up your negative beliefs. This step is the reason so many people have had great successes through this system. It's not about forcing yourself to make changes; it's about mastering something within by changing an underlying negative belief (under the watchful and supportive eye of your chosen animal) in order to clearly and definitively begin experiencing internal and external growth. Let me be very clear: this has nothing to do with willpower. It's about the results that begin to occur as you learn the lesson your animal has been diligently working to teach you. Finally, your dog isn't peeing in the house as much, or your horse is getting along better with his stall mate than he was a couple weeks ago, or the pig you've grown to love is letting go of her anxiety and playing with the other pigs.

Step 4: The Decision-Making Process

In this phase of the process you'll be asked to become your own little fortune-teller. But don't worry, this isn't as hard as it might sound, and it certainly doesn't require any psychic abilities. You'll simply use what you've learned about yourself and the special animal in your life to cull out moments that you can use for your new decision-making process. This is an exciting step in the process because it's a very active one. Most of what you've been doing thus far in the process is about observing, and now you'll be asked to put your new observation skills to work.

Step 5: Mastery

The fifth and final step is also exciting because it relates directly to subtle changes that are now happening within. Your deeply held negative beliefs about yourself—beliefs that are patently untrue (everyone deserves support and is worthy of love, but many people struggle to believe this, for example)—have been getting chipped away bit by bit through the Animal Lesson work. Here, you finally begin experiencing your life through a positive filter, instead of the old negative one, because the work you've done with this important animal has shown you a different reality. As a result, your decision-making processes are different, the animal you're working with is behaving differently, your environment is different, and how you feel about yourself is different. All these changes result in new, desired experiences in your life. This part of the process is not just about noticing the changes that have occurred—it's about living them. The transformations can be so deep that they just feel regular. Since there is no "push" or "force" to the changes (they have occurred within rather than through willpower), they have become the norm.

This system is not challenging. In fact, many people and their animal teachers successfully move through it in just a few weeks. Personally, I like that. I'm all for making things simple, easy, fun, and, yes … fast, while also improving the lives of the animals I do dearly love.

So, if you're ready to get going now, let's move into the details on how animals are really achieving these amazing results with humans around the world.

Setting the Stage

You're probably pretty excited to begin working with the special animal in your life and begin making changes within, but we're not going to jump right there yet. First, we have to set the stage so you can do the best Animal Lesson work possible.

Animal Emotions

Animals have complex emotions and senses, just like humans.

Your frame of mind is one of the most important factors for success with this system. Basically, you're going to have to wrap your head around and completely accept the idea that the animal you're choosing to focus on is as sensitive as you are and has a big-picture understanding of your personal world and the world in general. If you find this notion difficult to accept, you'll also find that moving through the process in this book will be difficult to accomplish. My advice: just go with it! If you don't believe it now, you surely will by the end of this book.

Every day our culture teaches us that animals are less intelligent than humans. You can see how that idea is reinforced as an almost universal belief in how we treat our animals around the world (just look at bull-fighting, factory farming, and circuses as a few examples). Luckily, there are many people who know differently, and their voices are becoming louder and louder as mass consciousness shifts from viewing animals as things without feelings to considering and treating them as beings with emotions and intelligence that rival, if not surpass, our own.

While working through this book, if you continue to discount what your animal is showing you ("How could an animal truly understand how I don't believe in myself?" or "It must be a coincidence"), you'll find yourself struggling. I was speaking with a client on the phone the other day about how I am writing this book on how people can experience incredible growth when they allow themselves to fully love an animal. His voice took on a serious tone as he told me about a study he'd read that concluded that the average adult dog's intelligence is equal to that of a three-year-old child. He then said, "But I don't agree with this at all!"

I laughed and said, "Neither do I!"

Before I could tell him how my work as an animal communicator had shown me that animals were, in many ways, more worldly, compassionate, intelligent, and understanding than most humans, he said, "I think it's more like a five-year-old child." The most interesting part of this conversation is not that this man views animals differently from me—it's that the conversation started because he wanted me to know how much he loves his dog Ralph and how Ralph had changed his life for the better by forcing him to be more active and meet more people in his neighborhood, a neighborhood he's lived in for over a decade. This man has already benefitted from the lesson his animal was teaching him—he just hasn't realized it yet!

What this client doesn't yet appreciate, and what many people in modern society don't yet appreciate, is that the way to gauge an animal's intelligence is not by asking that animal to figure out a contextual problem, by testing the animal's memory, nor any other method that is commonly used today. It is by looking at how animals live.

When you're feeling upset, does your cat slink over to you and sit by your side? When you're feeling lonely, does your dog suddenly drop a ball in your lap and start woofing to try and entice you to play? When you're feeling down in the dumps and go to the barn to visit the horses, does one horse immediately nuzzle you with loving kisses? When you're taking a walk through the woods and in a good mood, does it seem like the birds are singing to you?

Animals not only possess the capacity to understand the full range of our human emotions, they also possess the capacity to experience their own full range of emotions just as deep and turbulent as ours. Yes, you read that correctly. Animals have the same emotions that people have. I know there are some people, even great animal lovers like the client I just mentioned, who don't yet grasp this, but it's what I have witnessed every day working with animals and people, and it's what I believe you will come to realize to the core of your being as you make your way through this book. It's not a coincidence that when you're feeling lonely, your dog shows up and asks you to play. Your dog understands and experiences your loneliness and is subsequently handing you a solution. It's hard to feel lonely when you're out in the yard throwing the ball again and again with your dog, who is fully enveloping himself in the moment with you, loving, running, barking, and playing.

Animals are so clued in to our human emotions that they often take those emotions into themselves. As an animal communicator, countless people have brought their dog or cat or rabbit or cow to me because they were worried the animal was grieving the loss of his companion animal too hard. When I would intuitively connect in with the animal to ask about this though, I would most often receive an answer that would stun the animal's people. Of course animals grieve the loss of a beloved animal companion because there are definitive daily changes and things that can no longer happen: the two can't sleep next to each other anymore, steal each other's food, or hunt together, for example. But what may surprise you is the deeper answer to what is usually going on.

More than likely, the animal will tell me that he's feeling sad because his humans are so sad. And while this is not what people usually want to hear (many would rather focus on helping cure their pet's sadness than on dealing with their own grief), understanding what is really going on can be a huge help. Wild animals are very perceptive at noticing changes in their world. Natural selection has hammered this into their DNA, in fact, but in the wild, it could keep an animal alive to notice the emotional changes of those around her. To that end, today's domesticated animals still do this.

My travels as an animal communicator have proven to me that no emotion (and therefore no situation) is too complex for an animal to understand. Animals have talked to me about sadness, worry, fear, and anxiety but also about longing, jealousy, excitement, anticipation, and wariness. If it's an emotion that we can feel, it's an emotion that an animal can experience as well. When you discount the emotions and perceptions of animals, you miss the point of how animals can assist you in your life, and it will be hard to accept the deep work the animal wants to do with you.

Making an Agreement

To do this work, imagine that you and the animal in your life have made an agreement to complete an assignment together.

I know it sounds a little crazy, but the easiest way to understand how to work with an animal in this way and how to have the most success with it is to consider yourself as having signed a contract with your animal. By this I mean you are connected to this animal: you will learn whatever you're supposed to learn, and the animal is, through this agreement, going to continue working with you until you "get" and master whatever that lesson is.

Let's now expand on this contract analogy. The agreement between you and your animal is based on a mutual goal regarding your own soul's growth. That goal could be that you finally learn to value yourself, that you finally break free of your fear of failure, or that you finally begin standing up for yourself. Whatever your goal is, that's the animal's goal as well. We'll get more into this in later chapters when you start looking at why this animal is in your life, but for now, just know that you're both working toward the same goal.

As a result of this relationship between the animal and you, the animal will do anything and everything in her power to get you to realize your goal. This is part of that contract and means that your animal could start aggressively barking, get wounded, misbehave, become sick, make you feel loved in a way you've never felt before, or inspire within you a desire to seek justice for others, for example. The list of methods an animal could use to help you realize your goal is actually endless. What the animal does in order to get your attention so that you start working toward your mutual goal will depend on what your goal is, what your animal is capable of, and what will make you finally sit up, take notice, and learn that lesson!

Let's use an example of a woman named Charlotte who is dealing with a high-strung deer in her backyard that keeps running anxiously at her when she tries to mow her backyard. While it doesn't work this way all the time, in this example, the deer is reflecting Charlotte's own anxiety back to her. Now, this may seem like a simple case of the wild deer picking up on Charlotte's anxiety and carrying it around, but there's a catch. Because Charlotte and the deer are working together toward a common goal through their assignment, if Charlotte doesn't start making headway with her worry, the deer will step up her charging. For example, instead of running anxiously at Charlotte when she comes into the backyard, the deer may begin charging her, or perhaps she'll take things even further and start butting the sliding door window.

When you're in a situation like this with an animal, the animal is going to pull out all the stops necessary to get you to sit up and take notice. The goal of stepping things up a notch is to make things *so* uncomfortable (or in some cases so over-the-top amazing) that Charlotte feels that she has no choice but to start paying attention. And yes, this means if you try and ignore the situation, something about it will grow and grow until it almost becomes so overwhelming that you feel you must address it.

There is a massive positive side, though, to these human/animal contract relationships: once Charlotte starts tending to her anxiety, the deer will respond accordingly. Maybe Charlotte starts taking a meditation class or dumps the boyfriend who was creating all the challenges, which calms her anxiety down. Then perhaps she and the deer will be able to coexist in the backyard, for example. Whatever positive changes Charlotte makes will be reflected positively in the deer as well, as per the unspoken agreement the two have.

Dissecting How Animal Lessons Work

There are three main components to every human-animal relationship, regardless of the situation of the animal (i.e., the animal could be your pet, a neighbor's pet, a farm animal, a wild animal, or an animal you've only heard about). These are the *how*, the *what*, and the *work-arounds*.

- The *how* is the method the animal uses to bring something to your attention, such as barking, biting, inspiring you, charging you, or causing fear.
- The *what* is the deep lesson that animal is helping you learn, such as believing that you're lovable, good, whole, deserving, or safe.
- The *work-arounds* are the methods you've developed over time to help you avoid learning those lessons, such as trying to stay under the radar, not speaking up, or being overly competitive.

Let's break things down in the simplest way possible to begin. Usually, when I explain those three pieces to a client, they immediately construct a statement summarizing the relationship with the animal in their life. I call it the Animal Lesson Statement, and here is a typical example from one of my clients:

• •

My dog Stella is teaching me to love myself.

• •

With this statement, my client has deciphered what Stella is helping her learn: to love herself. This is a great starting point, but the statement is missing the how (what method the animal is using to teach this lesson) and the work-arounds (what my client does to avoid learning this lesson through the animal).

Determining the how is important: after all, how can you work on changing something if you don't know how it works? It may seem obvious when I lay it out like this, but despite this clarity, most people will initially lay out their Animal Lesson Statements and completely forget the how! Often this happens because a person is avoiding looking deeper at the relationship.

If you think you might be one of those people, you should feel encouraged. Your avoidance means your animal is tapping into something hidden within you that bears investigation! As you delve further into this process, those hidden emotions or thoughts that you've been trying to ignore will pop up despite how much you'd rather they don't—which is a part of the process I love. You can't hide anything from the animal in your life!

Here's an example of an Animal Lesson Statement that contains the what, the how, and the work-arounds:

. . . .

My dog Stella is teaching me to believe
I am strong and powerful by acting scared and overly
submissive every time I am feeling insecure
and trying to avoid being noticed.

. . . .

Aha! This statement explains things much more thoroughly. Now, both the what component (teaching her to believe she is strong and powerful) and the how component (by behaving a certain way) are included. This makes it easier to see the cause-and-effect relationship in play and better explains the human-animal relationship because the person has demonstrated not only what she is working on learning through her animal, but also the specific methods the animal is employing to get her attention and help her grow within.

There is still one element we haven't discussed yet, though: the work-arounds. Work-arounds are the behaviors and emotions we develop as a way to avoid having to deal with those inner lessons. A person who doesn't feel safe in the world may develop the work-around of trying to hide from others so that they don't notice her. Or a person who feels insecure may develop the work-around of trying to prove what a great person he is by striving to beat everyone out at his work.

In the example statement above, the work-around for my client is that whenever she feels insecure, she becomes submissive and small, thereby letting someone else take the credit for her work. Work-arounds can be so sneaky that you don't even notice them! What is most exciting about work-arounds? The animal in your life will always call you out on them! (But more about that later.)

We've now dissected the human-animal relationship through the what, the how, and the work-arounds in order to give you a foundation from which to work as you move through the rest of this book. So many people get all excited about working with an animal in this way that they skim over the significance of at least one of these aspects and end up working with their animal at a level that doesn't go nearly as deep as it could.

Animals are touching your life, not to help you get better at leash work, to force you to be a better trainer, or to push you into managing your temper, but to assist you in changing that belief within you that makes you choose to stop trying to get your dog to walk properly on the leash or the other part of you that chooses to prioritize everyone else above yourself. There is so much depth to what your animal understands about you that you're doing yourself a disservice if you don't find that depth in the relationship between the two of you.

Animals in Action: Melissa the Vet

I first met Melissa more than a decade ago. My assistant at that time was dividing her day between working for me and working as a vet tech for this "really amazing veterinarian" that she never stopped talking about. I wasn't overwhelmed with love for the vet that we had been working with for our dogs, Bella and Kelso, so we decided to try her out. For our first visit, Kevin and I brought both Bella and Kelso together—and this is when they were young and super rambunctious—so it was quite a chaotic visit. Despite all the disorder, as soon as I met Melissa I knew there was something very special about her. Her care for my dogs and for the other animals that visited her practice clearly came from her huge heart. Kevin loved that she took the time to talk with us about our dogs and demonstrated interest in getting to know each one of them. To this day, all my dogs have seen Melissa as their friend and vet. She not only understands the deeper connection between an animal and a person, she lives it.

When you learn that Melissa grew up on a farm in southern Minnesota, her unique love of animals may not seem to make sense at first. Melissa's family had what she calls an outdated mentality that ignored the animals' personal feelings: the animals were grown for food and for money, and if that animal wasn't going to produce either of those, then the animal had no value. In Melissa's own words, dogs and cats in particular were considered meaningless, as they did not contribute to putting dinner on the table. Melissa's view of animals, however, was very different from this.

As a child, once Melissa made the connection between what she was eating and the animals on the farm, she immediately decided to become vegetarian. For her, it didn't make sense to eat those creatures that she watched give birth, that she fed, cared for, and played with. Melissa's father couldn't understand her choices around animals and often thought she was just "full of nonsense," but rather than deter Melissa from these thoughts, this made her beliefs only grow stronger.

Because cats and dogs were not valued on the farm, they weren't spayed or neutered and weren't given vaccinations (as this was before the distemper vaccination was invented). This meant that many of the kittens and puppies born would die before they ever got a chance to mature. Melissa was especially drawn to the kittens and learned a lot about how to help them and keep them feeling comfortable just by spending the amount of time with them that she did. She would call her friends, who all lived in town in the suburbs, to come out to the farm and she would teach them all about the kittens.

Young Melissa developed a little test to tell the healthy kittens from the kittens that were going to die. If she put the kitten on his back and he could hold his head up, she knew that kitten would be strong enough to make it. If the kitten couldn't keep his head up, she knew he would die, and she'd do everything she could to help keep the sickly kittens comfortable until they passed away.

She'd known almost since she was a toddler that she wanted to be a veterinarian, but it was caring for those dying kittens that really guided her determination in pursuing her dreams. Every time a kitten died, Melissa was hugely affected. Each death fortified her determination to fulfill her veterinarian dream despite the beliefs of her father. This drove her to take her first job in research. Her plan had been to find that cure for distemper (which is what was killing the kittens), but since the vaccine had already been created by that time, she set about working on the vaccine for feline leukemia. The vaccine that she helped invent has now saved the lives of millions of cats worldwide.

Melissa's veterinary practice works with both domestic animals as well as birds and exotics. Her life growing up with the animals taught her that all animals, whether or not they earn money or produce food for the owner, are valuable, and that is certainly reflected in her practice today. It's no coincidence that she had to go against her father's wishes to assist the dying kittens, and today she's open to many different modalities for healing the animals she comes in contact with.

I'm sure that, no matter what, Melissa was destined to become a veterinarian. All those litters of kittens dying helped solidify her desires so that she could leave her old life behind to follow her dreams. She continues to help millions of animals every year, and the kittens helped her create a practice that I am proud to be a part of.

Chapter Two

THE LIFE CYCLE OF AN ANIMAL LESSON

At this early point, the process of working with an animal lesson may still seem a bit foreign to you, but I can assure you it's not. In my many years of doing this work, I've found this kind of work actually follows a pattern. I've seen person after person follow mostly the same path in terms of learning what needs to be learned.

Working with your animal lesson can be an emotionally challenging experience. There are several stages to the work that most people go through. As you move through this work with your animal, you will inevitably experience some type of resistance ("I don't want to learn that!") as well as acceptance ("Okay, I see that this is something that has been plaguing me for a long time."), and then excitement when things begin to shift ("Oh wow! This has never happened this way before!").

Whatever stage you find yourself in, don't judge it. If you're resisting or if things are finally moving forward smoothly, it's all just part of mastering this beautiful idea that your animal wants you to get. If you accepted it easily, right from the start, wouldn't you have already gotten the lesson? So no self-judgments here, no beating yourself up, no wishing it were faster or easier or wishing it were something else other than what it is.

You'll hear me say this again and again, but this work is not hard. The only real challenge is your commitment to it as you move through the various phases. Just keep your eye on your special animal, and eventually things will fall into place. Now, let's move out of the emotional shifts that will go on and look at how animal lessons play out from a higher perspective.

The Beginning

Do you ever feel like a particular animal chose you? Or have you ever felt drawn to a certain animal? My work with tens of thousands of animals and their people has taught me that animals deliberately choose the humans they interact with. Of course that means that your favorite horse (the horse that just makes your heart sing) chose you as her human, but it also means that your mom's dog, whom you became the caretaker of when your mom passed away and whom you find infinitely annoying, also chose you. Additionally, the fox that you almost hit with your car as he darted across the highway chose you too. All these animals have something to teach you through your interaction with them, whether that interaction is brief or a lifelong adventure.

In your human-animal relationships, once you and the animal have come together in some way, the learning begins! Now, "come together" could mean once this animal starts to live with you in your house, but it's certainly not limited to this. The animal you are coming together with could be your neighbor's cat, whom you've never even touched, the new lamb born to one of your favorite sheep, or even a wild animal you read about on social media. The human-animal relationship is not limited to pets—it extends out to any and every animal you are moved by, have an emotional experience with (whether positive or negative), or come into contact with.

Now, what's even more interesting about these relationships is that one animal does not necessarily have the same thing to teach every human he comes into contact with (although, sometimes that is actually the case). Let's look at an aggressive family dog, for example. The aggressiveness the dog holds may be a way for him to teach Laura how to chill out, to help Laura's partner Jill learn to be more aggressive, to help the oldest daughter in the family to stand up for herself, and to teach the youngest daughter to become more aware of her surroundings. These human-animal relationships are totally and completely personalized!

Lesson Methods

In a human-animal relationship, you must deal with the challenges (positive or negative) that arise in order to uncover what that animal is there to teach you. Your job is then to learn this lesson! Unlike what most animal trainers would say, your role in your human-animal relationship is always going to be to "do" you, because change won't happen (no matter how badly you want it to) until you do.

These special relationships tend to work in one of a few ways. Although the content within the relationship may change from relationship to relationship, the methods for getting the work done on the animal's part usually fall into one of four categories.

Mirroring

This is probably the easiest to recognize in a human-animal relationship. Some animals will choose to mirror the behavior of the person (or of their environment) as a way to point out the area in which learning needs to happen. This goes back to how an anxious human often lives with an anxious cat, for example, but it is certainly not limited to that, as it could be extended out to feeling a great anxiety and worry for an anxious elephant located on the other side of the world. Other mirroring could be a horse who doesn't have confidence out in the field because the human doesn't have confidence out in the field. A dog that doesn't like men who is mirroring her human who doesn't trust men.

Modeling

Sometimes an animal will behave in the exact opposite manner of the person involved in order to make a point. Common examples of this are the high-strung human with the very low-energy, relaxed, lazy dog or the cat obsessed with cleanliness in the house of the man who is a hoarder. Animals often perfect the behavior that the person involved is struggling to achieve. I've also worked with animals that will model a behavior to the extreme, such as a dog that is modeling confident behavior so thoroughly that the behavior moves into aggression.

Producing New Emotions

This type of relationship most often shows up in a positive way, but that doesn't mean it's any easier to navigate. I often see this occur with cats. The cat will be the most supportive, dependable being in a person's life, radiating unconditional love for the human. Now, while this seems wonderful, usually the humans who find themselves with this type of relationship have a hard time accepting that love or finding it anywhere other than with their special cat, or they have a belief that the only one who could ever be that supporting and accepting of them would be their cat.

Sickness/Disease

Some people find this form of relationship very upsetting, but I must talk about it because it's common. Some animals will develop a sickness, and that sickness can be used as a learning tool for the human involved. For example, it's possible that someone who never takes any time for himself, works eighty hours a week, and doesn't have a personal life will end up with a dog that has a broken leg or a wild rabbit or bird that requires around-the-clock medical care. The animal's goal in this situation may be to teach that person how to slow down and smell the flowers (which they will have to do in order to care for the animal) and stop pressing to be the best all the time. Now, this doesn't mean that all sicknesses in animals are signs that we need to slow down, just in this example. But I have often seen this play out. When an animal has a medical problem, if the human changes his lifestyle, mindset, expectations of life, emotions, or something else big (depending on the lesson), things will often alleviate for that animal. I do want to point out though that I use the word "alleviate" on purpose because alleviate does not always mean that the animal stops being sick; it could also mean that the animal crosses over or some other option.

Lesson Completion

This brings me to the big question that everyone asks me when they first learn about these special human-animal relationships: "What happens when you finally master the lesson this animal has been working so hard to teach you?" After all, if you're in this theoretical contract with the animal, there has to be an ending, right? The answer is actually very simple, although many people fear it. When you finally master this soul-level, heart-expanding thing about yourself that this animal has been working so hard to get you to see, there is no longer a need for that animal to remain part of your life. That means the animal could pass over, he could go to live with another family, he could run away, you could unexpectedly not be able to take care of him anymore, or any other number of options. The relationship only lasts as long as it takes you to learn and master a particular deep truth about yourself.

Now, I know that no one likes this aspect of the work, but I have seen it play out time and time again. It means that, when an animal does leave your life, a great lesson has been had within you. But to many people, even the thought of the loss of the animal they are connected to can make doing this relationship work completely unacceptable. At this point, most people will say to me (or at least think to themselves), "Alrighty then, I'm not going to do this work! I'd rather not learn the lesson than take the risk of losing my beloved dog/cat/chicken/zebra, etc." Please avoid saying this!

So many of us get so attached to the animals in our lives—whether they're our domesticated cats and dogs, our farm animals, the wild animals living near our home, or simply an animal we've heard about on the news or through social media—but this is a fact of life and of this deep work with animals. When the animal has done his or her job and taught the lesson, the animal will take her leave, and my intuitive work with animals has shown me again and again that this is a good thing. Animals enjoy moving on to the next stage of their evolution!

Humans are a funny lot. When everything is wonderful in our lives, we don't really do much to make changes. No one wakes up in the morning and says, "I love my life, my job, my family, and how everything is going so perfectly right now. Because of that, I'm going to change it all up!" No. When things are good, many of us can get complacent or spend our time trying to ensure that things stay exactly as they are. It's when things are bad or challenging or difficult that we tend to make changes, because that's when we're open to change. Here's where you have to give animals their due: the animal in your life is going to see through you. Yup. And are you starting to clue into what happens then yet?

Things get *big*. Life gets tougher. The challenge gets bigger.

Let's look at Rachel the aggressive pig and her human, Ferris. Ferris has decided that he doesn't want to do his work with Rachel the aggressive pig because he has too many other things on the farm that he feels he should be focusing on and doesn't have time to relax, which is what Rachel has been showing him he needs to do. So, instead of learning how to chill out, he continues to push himself harder and harder to get everything on the property done properly. Well, as a result of Ferris ignoring his work with Rachel the pig, Rachel may then choose to become *more* aggressive, perhaps even fighting with the other pigs. Or maybe she'll get very sick, to force Ferris to slow down and take care of her. Rachel the pig will do whatever she can possibly do that will get Ferris's attention. And you can be sure that Rachel will not choose something that Ferris can easily overlook; she'll make things harder and more challenging until Ferris finally feels that he has no choice but to listen and learn how to relax.

This deep learning and growing can also happen directly through an animal's passing. Military dogs' funerals are often highlighted in social media. These highly trained dogs have usually saved countless lives through their military service and are often overlooked at the end of their life when they can no longer perform their duties. There are many organizations working to help match up these dogs with their handlers from when they were on active duty. When a military dog dies, often there is a public funeral honoring the work of this dog. For many, this is an opportunity to remember the unconditional love of this animal who served so faithfully, and I have witnessed many hearts opening as a result of these funerals. Sometimes, a passing doesn't indicate that a lesson has come to its culmination, sometimes the passing *is* the lesson itself.

Instead of worrying about what happens to the animal at the completion of these complicated yet unconditionally loving human-animal relationships, I invite you to enjoy the relationship all the way through. From challenge to challenge, success to success, lesson to lesson, your relationship with the special animal in your life is there to be witnessed (and enjoyed) by you, and working deeply with your animal in this way will make the relationship even more pleasurable.

Animals in Action:
Danielle's Lesson from the Dolphins

My quiet, introverted husband actually laughed out loud at what I'd just said. "You're going to take a group of people on a dolphin swim?" he asked.

"Yes," I said very seriously while looking him directly in the eye. "Yes, I am."

"You're going to get in the water?"

"Yes…" But I could feel my determination waning a little bit.

"And swim in the open ocean?"

"Yes…" And now I wasn't so sure.

Kevin had been asking me these questions with good reason. For the past fifteen years I had made sure to stay out of any body of water other than a pool. So, to him, it seemed like a tall order (and perhaps in his mind a supremely stupid order) for me to book myself to lead a group of thirteen people on a wild dolphin swim in the middle of the open ocean in Bimini, Bahamas. While I was happy to ride on a boat or paddle around on a kayak, I did everything I could to avoid actually submerging my body in the water. My one water-skiing adventure had resulted in my friends believing I was an expert water-skier because I didn't fall once. This was out of sheer fear, not skill. I was *not* going into that water.

My phobia began more than a decade and a half earlier on our belated honeymoon in Kauai. Kevin and I had booked a snorkeling trip on a large catamaran with about fifty other people. It was only a day trip, and the captain of the boat took us around the island to various beautiful spots, where we would snorkel to view the fish, plants, and lots of other little swimmy critters. I'd always been somewhat fearful of things touching my legs while in the water, but it had never kept me from swimming. However, on that fateful day in Kauai, this was all about to change.

At the first snorkel spot things went well, despite my hesitation. The area was protected by a coral reef and the number of fish both large and small was almost overwhelming, but with Kevin there it was more interesting than scary. Kevin and I reveled in the beautiful colors and spent a lot of time motioning to one another with pointed fingers under water to "come see this!"

The second snorkel spot, however, was different. It was in a protected cove that was shallower than the open ocean but much larger than the first spot. Land was far away, so the only way to get out of the water was to climb back up on the boat with the helping hand of the captain or one of the crew. I was feeling a little unsure, so while everyone else spread out fifty or so feet away from the boat, I hugged the side and kept pulling Kevin toward me. He wasn't happy about that, as he tends to like to explore more than I do, but after five years together, he'd come to accept some of my little idiosyncrasies and was happily supporting me.

We were feeling complete with our adventure, so Kevin climbed back up on the boat first in order to help me out of the water. As I waited for him to get in position, my legs felt somewhat vulnerable because of all the fish swimming around and because Kevin was no longer there to protect me. But all in all, I was okay because I knew I was about to get out of the water and back onto the boat. While I was waiting, the captain jokingly decided to dump a huge bowl of bread pieces into the water all around me.

Well, if you know anything about fish, you know that they're going to love that bread! I spent the next five minutes in pure panic as one fish after another nipped for the food surrounding my body in the water. I could feel little fish mouths touching me, gently swimming all around me, unafraid of my body, and it was more than I could handle. I felt utterly helpless there in the open water, being mowed all over by hungry fish, and there was nothing I could do to control the situation until I was out of the water. Unfortunately, Kevin had not yet realized what was going on, as he was putting his fins and snorkel away, and I was left in an almost panic-attack state. Finally, I was able to grab the side of the boat, and with a burst of strength I hoisted myself up and landed my bum on the boat floor, without help from anyone else. (It's amazing the strength that adrenaline provides!) Needless to say, I was not happy with the captain.

In the subsequent fifteen years, going into the ocean or a lake felt too uncontrollable. Since I couldn't always see what was in the water that would potentially touch me, it never felt safe for me to venture in. So my honeymoon in Kauai was the last time I had entered any body of water other than the pool in my backyard until my swim with the wild dolphins.

Bimini. It was one of those things that I just decided to do. I had considered over ten different trips, but nothing appealed to me like the wild dolphin trip. Although I didn't know much about dolphins, I'd always felt drawn to them. On my desk, I had a small dolphin statue that I liked to hold between my fingers while I meditated, and I had spent time listening to YouTube clips of dolphins chatting between one another. So, without really acknowledging my fear of the water, I gave the okay and had my event organizer schedule wild dolphins for August. Perhaps it was weird to schedule leading a trip that would center on my greatest phobia, but since I wasn't acknowledging that I even had that phobia, it was actually easy to agree.

As I know now, I was already being guided by the dolphin energy. And what I learned served to solidify my belief in the greater purpose of animals here on earth and helped me release a great portion of my own deep-seated belief that I am not safe in the world. Yes, all this happened because of the dolphins!

First, let me make clear that this was a wild dolphin situation, and I would never have agreed to do this with dolphins in captivity. I believe dolphins should be free, and swimming with wild dolphins is very different from encountering them in a captive situation.

Each afternoon on the trip, our group would drive the boat ten miles out into the middle of the ocean with our steady captain to call upon the dolphins. Luckily for us, dolphins are attracted to boats, to people, and to happy snorkelers, so if we made ourselves known, the dolphins would usually follow soon after. They were not trained to do this; instead they were as drawn to us as we were to them. It was their choice to play with us, and if they made that choice, it was also up to them to determine what that play looked like. Sometimes they would interact with each snorkeler, coming so close that people would have to pull their arms and legs in so the dolphins wouldn't run into them, while other days the dolphins would decide they wanted to put on a show.

When I went into this trip, I didn't know anything about how the dolphins would behave. In fact, as the days approached, all I could think of was how susceptible I would feel scooting my bum off the back of the boat into the open ocean—and how much potential there was for fish to touch my legs (or bite my legs) as I swam. At the same time, I was also plagued by the realization that I was the group leader. If I showed this fear, it would set a negative tone for the entire trip, and that was not something I wanted to do.

But if there was anything that my work with animals had taught me, it was to listen to that little voice inside me that said, "Do it anyway."

It took about an hour and a half on the boat, searching the ocean and making our presence known, for the dolphins to show up on that day. While everyone else was excited, I immediately felt a sense of dread. Now that the dolphins had arrived, I was going to have to lead the group into the murky, cold water, and I was going to have to do it all with a smile on my face so that no one would know the true depths of my fear.

As I slipped each foot into a fin, my hands started shaking, and I felt challenged, taking a full breath into my lungs. I found myself hoping that the shaking was related to excitement, even though I knew it was due to fear. I'd already been in the water once with the dolphins the day prior, but luckily I had been forced to hoist myself back on the boat due to three snorkel malfunctions. For that first swim, equipment malfunctions turned out to be my friend and saved me from having to confront the depths of the ocean. But this time around, my snorkel had been fixed and there was no reason for me, as the group leader, not to go into the water.

Now, I've been working to bridge the gap of understanding between animals and humans for many years. And in all that time, the most important thing I've learned is that, in *everything* they do, animals are always teaching and assisting humans. Was I thinking about this as I got ready to slide into the water? No. But luckily the dolphins were.

I decided that I could talk myself into changing my fear of the open ocean. I consciously told myself, "You're okay, Danielle. The dolphins will take care of you. You're totally safe and protected out here in the ocean because you're with these incredible animals."

But you'll find as you get further into this book that this is probably the least effective method for creating deep, soul-level change. Have you ever tried to convince yourself of something that your heart has a hard time believing? It doesn't work. Soul-growth does not come about through force and willpower. Instead, it comes through the change in beliefs. And no matter how much I told myself I was safe and didn't need control of the ocean to be safe, my belief was not going to change until I experienced that safety.

So I took the plunge (slowly) and gently lowered myself off the boat platform into the open water. Immediately my feet and legs felt exposed. *What is below me? What might slide by my legs? What if my legs touch seaweed or worse, get stuck in seaweed? What if … what if … what if?* My mind was racing as I doggy paddled a little ways away from the boat to (supposedly) find the dolphins.

I then proceeded to spend the next twenty minutes trying to control my situation. (Again, this is the opposite of what I am about to teach you.) *Where is the boat? Where is the group? Is the group together? How close am I to the edge of the group? Look*

down there; can something get me? Oh, and where are the dolphins?
That's a big wave—try to avoid those. Where'd the boat go now?
I felt that if I could keep everything in order and really control
what was going on, I would be safe. It was a careful dance of putting my head in the water to watch the legs of my group, lifting
my head to ensure the boat was nearby, putting my head back
into the water, and basically ignoring the dolphins.

Finally, the captain gave the hand signal indicating that the dolphins were moving on and we should swim back to the boat. I'm
sure it's no surprise that I was the first person back on the boat.

Several people stood around at the back of the boat in awe
of what they had just experienced. "Amazing!" and "Wow!" were
peppered about. I, on the other hand, was just happy to have my
breathing return to normal and to spend the next hour relaxing
at the front of the boat with the group, secure that I wouldn't
have to confront dolphins again until tomorrow. I was wrong.

Thirty minutes later, "We've got dolphins!" yelled the captain.
Oh, dear.

Once again, everyone traipsed back to the salon to don their
snorkeling gear. Once again, I felt that familiar shake and quake at
the thought of reentering the open ocean. In fact, compared to our
location earlier, we were now further out into the open ocean.

Five people left the boat before it was my turn. Finally, I gin-
gerly slid into the water. As I adjusted my mask and snorkel to
match the contours of my face, I noticed that a dolphin jumped
out of the water not three feet from my face. Whoa! Rather than
feeling scared, I felt intrigued, which was a very different emotion. After the last encounter, those who had come this close to
these wonderful beings seemed to be entranced. I wanted to experience that, and after one jumped right in front of me ... well, I
wanted to see more.

I quickly put my face in the water and looked around. My breathing was loud through the snorkel, but for the time being it was the only thing I could hear above the *rrrrrr* of the boat's motor. The dolphin was right there in front of me! He swam about ten feet away from me, and then he turned around and headed straight toward me. Just before he would have hit me, he slowed down and swam by to my right. I watched him as he watched me with one big, beautiful eye, and then he was gone, playing with his friends about fifteen feet away.

Wow! I thought to myself. *I want more of this.* It felt as if he were looking right at me, calling me to him. He was so close that if he had eyelashes, I would have seen them.

I quickly began to paddle toward another three dolphins that were swimming in a little group together. As I approached, they seemed to sense I was there and wanted me to join them. They surrounded me as they swam past me, and then they swam back and repeated the game. I made sure to keep my hands and legs to myself so as not to get in their way, but I also made sure to keep the dolphins in my sights. I felt drawn to them, and the more I concentrated on them, the easier it was to be with them.

Our group kept playing with the dolphins like this for more than thirty minutes. A few of the dolphins would swim toward me and then away from me, and they even put on a show for us. They would gather into a group of four or five, and together they would gracefully dive thirty feet down toward the white sandy bottom. In unison, they would turn around and shoot up toward the surface. I was utterly mesmerized, and they would all pop out of the water at once, only to land with a splash, still in formation. It was like I was watching my own private dolphin dance. It felt as if they had let me into their safe, playful world. And all that mattered to me was staying there with them and with our group. Even as I write this now, I can feel their pull, their serenity, and their comfort. It was the ultimate feeling of "everything is all right, right now." Amazingly, I stopped worrying about how far away the boat was, where the other snorkelers were, or how exposed I was to the rest of the ocean. There was something about communing with the dolphins that allowed me to let go of all my fears. It was like a kind of universal protection in one of the most unprotected spaces. I knew I had nothing to worry about, nothing to control, nothing to look over, and nothing to make happen. All I had to do was just be.

Afterward, as I sat on the edge of the boat, reliving the experience, I realized that the dolphins had beautifully acted as my teacher. Much like my trainer at the gym will show me how to do a proper front squat, the dolphins were training me in feeling secure in the world. When I let go of my need to control things, to control my environment, to manage where the boat and all the people were, I was able to relax right into the experience I was having. I was finally free to experience the world as the safe place that it is.

Control is something that I have struggled with throughout my life. As a child, I developed the belief that control was the antidote to my lack of safety. Because I didn't feel safe growing up, I leaned on controlling my environment, my situation, and the people around me as best as I could. At least that way I would know what was coming at me, and I could be prepared for whatever scary, unsafe thing it was.

By viewing the dolphins as my trainers and accepting that they had something to teach me, I was actually able to let go of control throughout the rest of the trip. The more I went with the flow, the happier I felt. Sure, I was still the group leader, but I was also immersed in a world that I really couldn't control. Through the dolphins, I learned that that is okay with me; I will still be safe, supported, and protected.

The dolphins helped me to master a long-held belief I've had about myself (that I'm not safe or supported in the world), *and* they gave me the incredible boost of actually experiencing what letting go feels like. Animals are always working at this bigger, deeper level to help people see within themselves what is holding them back, and my time with the dolphins was indicative of this.

I only swam with the dolphins on four afternoons, and yet the impact they made on my life was enormous. Now, imagine what you can experience as a result of working with your own pet, whom you see every single day of your life! The possibilities for healing, moving forward, changing your life, and creating your life are limitless when you are willing to explore the animal as your teacher, mentor, trainer, and guru.

Chapter Three

STEP 1: DETERMINE HOW YOUR ANIMAL IS HELPING YOU

I'm sure you're ready to get going, and it's finally time! I love that animals assist us the way they do, and the more people do this work with the animals in their life, the more we'll be able to change the way people around the globe understand their relationship with the animal world and, in response to that, hold compassion for one another. It took me a long time to completely believe that this was true, though, and my goal is to help people align with this fact a whole lot faster than I did. As a child, I wasn't exposed to other people's stories of how having an animal could shift a person's life for the better because there was no Internet, and news stories in the paper or on TV only focused on such events when they were in search of a "feel-good" story. Today, however, through social media, we're practically bombarded with goodwill tales about people and animals joining together and the resulting transformations. Until now, though, harnessing that power was elusive: it was more something that people realized only after the animal had already changed their lives. With this book, you're being given the information and the power to consciously enter into the relationship with your animal with your eyes wide open, ready to foster that transformation.

Choose the Best Animal to Work With

The first thing to know about choosing the best animal to work with is that you can't make a wrong choice here. That's right— you can't make a mistake! Chances are that you picked up this book because you had a particular animal in mind that you wanted to deepen your relationship with, that you wanted to understand, or that you are being troubled by. If that's the case for you, that's wonderful, and you should definitely stick with that animal.

If you're someone who has a connection to many animals, remember that each animal is your teacher in its own way. If you have four dogs, two horses, three cats, and you've "adopted" an elephant in India, know they are undoubtedly all working to assist you in your evolution in some way. Each animal does not necessarily have the same agenda with you, but each animal is helping you one way or another. This is also the case for the wild animals or other animals you're concerned with. Each beautiful being is aiding you according to his or her abilities and how the two of you come together on emotional, physical, energetic, and mental levels, and this may or may not be linked to how other animals are assisting you. Your goal in this moment is to decide which animal is the teacher you'll be concentrating most on for now. You can go back and do the process again and again and again with your other animals as well, but let's keep things simple for now and pick just one.

To decide which of the animals in your life will be best to start with, I encourage you to look to the animal that is creating the greatest waves on a daily basis. This could mean it's the dog that is upsetting you with his aggressiveness, the ferret that is biting all the children in the classroom, the cat that is showing you the kind of love you've never felt before, or the sheep that, whenever you see her out in the field, gives you the biggest "feelies." The greatest waves idea includes both the positive and negative emotions. You'll want to choose the animal that is creating the greatest waves for you because, unlike how the rest of the world works, the bigger the wave, the more content for you to work with, the easier it is to evolve and grow through this work! Choosing the greatest-wave animal may seem counterintuitive, as you would think that a smaller wave would indicate the work will be easiest, but in the animal world, things are reversed. Which animal do you have the most "stuff" with? Think of that animal and get ready to go for it!

Once you've chosen your greatest wave animal, you're ready to get going. And remember, you can go through this process again for another animal in the future—and by then you'll be an expert, so it will be even easier!

Identify How This Animal Is Working with You

I'm sure that, as you've been reading, you've been defining and redefining what you think the relationship between you and your animal must be. It's kind of fun, isn't it? How is my pet helping me? How is the chipmunk in the backyard teaching me? I love helping people figure this part of their animal relationship out because, no matter how much of an animal lover someone is, they are almost always blown away when they realize the profound depths animals are willing to go to for them.

A lot of understanding the how with your animal comes by looking at yourself first. Start remembering the thoughts, feelings, ideas, and emotions you've had about this animal in the past. It doesn't matter if your past thoughts and feelings were positive, negative, or a mix of both. Consider, as well, what others who've known that animal (dog walker, veterinarian, farrier, rehabilitation professional, handler, neighbor, etc.) have had to say about her and how that made you feel. If you've chosen an animal you've never met (such as the bottlenose dolphin you heard about on the Internet and felt so moved by), think back to the descriptions you've read or heard about this animal and what emotions you felt through those descriptions. Don't worry about what these things mean, don't judge yourself for feeling them, and try not to censor anything that comes up. Just simply remember how you've thought and felt about this animal while this animal has been a part of your life. Simply, think about the different facets of your relationship from this new, purely emotional perspective.

Unlike what many in our society would have us believe, emotions are not annoying things that get in the way of our day, hindering us from achieving great success. They are indicators that something is going on within us and that that something, whatever it is and where it is coming from, warrants our attention. No one wakes up in the morning feeling happy, calm, and peaceful and decides to change their whole life. Instead, waking up feeling upset, dissatisfied, fearful, excited, or annoyed is much more likely to push us to do things differently. And our animals are greatly aware of this fact: they know that by eliciting enough strong emotions within us, we will eventually take action.

Now, from this newly activated place of feeling about your animal, take a moment to answer these questions. Please be as honest as you can, even if you are embarrassed or upset by what arises for you. The more raw and uncensored you are here, the easier it will be for you to figure out what's really going on with you and this special animal. Record your answers, even if just in the margins of this book, so that it's harder to censor yourself. Your reply can be either positive or negative, since one type of answer is not better than another; each answer is merely a clue.

- When you think of this animal, what is the first emotion you feel?
- When you think of this animal, what is the second emotion you feel?
- When you think of this animal, what is the third emotion you feel?
- (If applicable) When you hang around with this animal for a while, how do you end up feeling during this time? Afterward?
- (If applicable) When you read/hear about this animal, how do you end up feeling during this time? Afterward?
- When you're not around this animal or don't have contact with this animal for an extended period of time, what emotions do you feel?
- Do your feelings about this animal ever change? If so, from what to what?

Answering these questions as truthfully as you can is important because that truth is what will help you ferret out the sometimes-hidden sentiments buried within the relationship that you may be overlooking. To receive the most from this relationship, you must be aware of all its aspects, including (and most importantly) the parts that you may not want to deal with. This means that, even though you love your cat dearly, your initial emotional responses to these questions may be negative, perhaps because of some challenge you're experiencing with her, and that's okay. If this is the case for you, don't beat yourself up—congratulate yourself for being so honest! Those preliminary emotions are raw and real, and they are *the* signs you're looking for to the inner workings of your human-animal relationship. These sentiments regarding your chosen animal point to the fact that *something is going on,* and that something is going to be the crux of this relationship.

Take a look at the emotions you've just noted. Some of what you've recorded is going to be applicable to understanding this relationship, and some will not be. Are any of these emotions completely normal, par for the course, or something you feel often in your life? If yes, then simply cross those emotions off. For some people, an example of this would be love: I always love my dogs, and I'm used to feeling love for my dogs. I would then simply remove that from my emotion list if it came up as one of the answers to the questions above. Here, you want to discover and focus on the less common emotions because those are the emotions that will direct you toward what you're working on with your animal.

Next, are any of the emotions on your list caused by a particular challenge you're experiencing with your animal? If yes, then just place a circle around those emotions.

Are any of the emotions you wrote down something that you're not used to experiencing (whether positive or negative)? Is yes, then draw a big ol' circle around each one. Each time that unique emotion comes up, be sure to circle it again, even if it already has a circle. You're probably going to end up with at least one emotion circled a few times.

Are you upset or disturbed by any of the emotions on your list? For example, maybe you've been embarrassed to admit it, but one of the things your horse is making you feel is rage. This would be an emotion that, because of the embarrassment, deserves to be circled and also points out why it's so important to be honest as you're answering those questions above. If yes, circle the emotions that upset you as well.

By now, you should have a handful or so of emotions in front of you that you've circled several times. If there are any emotions on this list that you have not yet circled, you can put those to the side as well. At this point, the circled emotions are giving us the best clues about this human-animal relationship.

To help you along, here's an example of how someone could walk through the exercise: Jenny has chosen her dog Flower as her teacher for this work. When answering the questions above, the main emotions she felt when she thought of Flower were love, frustration, embarrassment, and anger. She immediately crossed the emotion "love" off her list because she was very used to experiencing love with the animals in her life. However, she ended up circling "anger" twice, "embarrassment" twice, and "frustration" three times. Jenny certainly has a lot of circles coming up at this point!

Now, without even knowing the details around what is going on between Jenny and Flower yet, it's easy to tell that *something* is happening based purely on the fact that Jenny has several circled emotions—otherwise, why would she be experiencing anger, embarrassment, and frustration with this animal? The circled emotions on your own list are the clues into understanding what area in your life your animal is working with. Think about the emotion you circled most. What is happening that is causing that emotion? Is there a particular event or events that conjure that feeling? Animals tend to work with people through repeated patterns because it seems that most people need to be hit over the head again and again before they will get what is going on. It's very possible, and even likely, that the emotion you've circled the most is something you feel again and again with your animal through a particular repeated experience.

Jenny circled "frustration" the most when answering the questions above. After looking at it for a moment, Jenny had a pretty good idea where that frustration was stemming from in her relationship with Flower: it was a particular thing that Flower often did. Flower was a terrible greeter of people in any situation. It didn't matter if someone was just walking by the front door of Jenny's house, approaching them on the sidewalk to say hi, or just running by—Flower's reaction was always the same: she would loudly and incessantly bark, and it felt to Jenny that nothing that she could do would deter Flower from that. Jenny felt that many people on her street were afraid of Flower and struggled several times a day to try to control this situation. Jenny concluded that experiences like this had resulted in her repeated experience of frustration with her dog. This lack of good greeting manners is how Flower is working with Jenny.

Like Jenny, your circled emotions will be related to a repeating pattern or experience with your animal. Remember, though, that that pattern doesn't have to be negative, as it was with Jenny and Flower. For example, one of the emotions you wrote down could have been "supported" because perhaps you've never before experienced the kind of love and devotion and consistent dependability that you're now experiencing with this animal through her following you around in your home. This experience counts as a repeated pattern as well, even though it's positive rather than negative. I've found that most human-animal relationships focus on a negative pattern rather than a positive one because that seems to be what more easily gets a person's attention. Just take note of what repeated experiences are creating these emotions with your animal, and *voilà*! You have found how your animal is helping you learn!

Beginning Your Animal Lesson Statement

Now that you've deciphered how your animal is getting your attention and you know what emotions are being brought up as a result, you're ready to make your own Animal Lesson Statement that summarizes this very special relationship. Putting the relationship into the statement form will help you see and understand what is going on. Let's use Jenny and Flower as an example.

Animal Lesson Statement Template

• •

_____ *(Animal name)*

is doing _____ *(how)*

to help me learn _____ *(what lesson)*

by making me feel _____ *(emotions)*

and therefore do _____ *(work-arounds).*

• •

Here's what we have for Jenny's statement so far:

• •

Flower is barking at everyone

to help Jenny learn _____

(what lesson) by making her feel embarrassed and frustrated

and therefore do _____ *(work-arounds).*

• •

We've identified how Flower is doing this (by barking at everyone and greeting them badly) and the emotions that this brings up in Jenny (frustration and embarrassment). Now, give it a try for yourself using the template.

Hooray! You're officially on your way to really figuring out this incredible relationship with your animal! Isn't it exciting to know that these behaviors you've identified in this animal are specifically there to help you learn a deeply held lesson about yourself? When you understand that what you're experiencing with your animal is the *result* of this extraordinary kind of relationship, intended to help you grow and expand (rather than be frustrated and angry, for example), it can automatically become a lot easier to exist within that relationship. It's not that your rabbit likes chaos or that the neighbor's parrot wants to make you pull your hair out—well, not exactly! There is a purpose and a point. This can feel like a great weight off your back. Finally, things are starting to make sense.

As you look at the partial Animal Lesson Statement you've just written out, you may have already been addressing this behavior or challenge with your animal, but most likely, you weren't achieving the intended results. This is because you were most likely working on the animal's behavior rather than the underlying lesson for you. After knowing how much more is taking place beneath the surface in your human-animal relationship, you're probably feeling like you can breathe a sigh of relief because change is in sight. The next chapter holds the fun part—figuring out the lesson behind all of this.

Animals in Action: John Holland and Koda

I first met psychic medium John Holland when he brought his dog, Koda, to me for an animal communication reading. John was having some challenges with Koda, and as a kind of last resort, he'd decided to try out an animal communicator. Despite being a psychic medium (a person who communicates psychically with our deceased human loved ones), he was unsure whether animals had any intuitive abilities. I was able to show him the light on that fact. That reading was the beginning of a beautiful friendship that has lasted years, but John's story with Koda really began several years earlier.

John is one of the most sensitive people I've ever met (and I'm surrounded by sensitive people every day). Over the years, he's honed his intuition beautifully to help him become the well-known psychic medium he is today. And as with all psychics, his sensitivity also extends to his personal life. After all, it's very challenging to be sensitive at work and then turn it off at home!

To help him heal from a challenging breakup, John dove headfirst into his work. He lived in a condominium in New England while traveling around the world demonstrating his extraordinary ability to connect with loved ones on the other side. The more he worked, the more it helped him heal his broken heart—but the more his heart healed, the lonelier he realized he was becoming. He rarely spent time at his condo, preferring instead to put his love and energy into building his career, not noticing that he didn't feel a connection to his house or to a community. For three years he concentrated on his work, and in that time grew to be even more successful than he already was.

But he knew something was missing.

Finally, John felt healed and prepared enough to bring a West Highland Terrier, which he named Koda, into his life. Little did John know that every single aspect of his life was about to change.

John does not lack commitment, and bringing a dog into his life was no different. He was going to do Koda right—no two bones about it. To that end, Koda required doggy day care, walks, and socialization. A lot of socialization. These were all things that John was unfamiliar with, as his recent life until that time had consisted of work and then some more work. With his travel schedule, John had to find a reputable doggy day care center, and after several tries, he finally came upon one he trusted. Next, he had to feel good about where Koda would be doing any boarding. It took a few months, but John was able to secure places that he felt good about and where he knew Koda would be in good hands.

One day early in their relationship, little Koda got loose and ran across the street into the neighbor's yard. Although John had lived in his condo for over three years, he really wasn't familiar with his neighbors. A nod hello or a quick wave was the extent of those relationships for him so far and that suited John fine, as he wasn't really thinking about putting down roots. But Koda had other plans. While frantically trying to secure Koda, John started talking with the neighbor about her Boston Terrier. The conversation was so interesting that he continued talking even after he'd gotten Koda under control. He didn't think about returning to work that whole afternoon.

As it turned out, the neighbors held a meetup every day in the yard so that their dogs could play. John loved how interested his neighbors were in this little being that had lit up his life, and he relished the chance to talk with people who understood his feelings for Koda. As the days wore on, John started joining the meetup groups. He said, "It's almost like I didn't have a choice, Danielle. He was going over there whether I took him or not!"

Today, John's neighbors have become his lifelong friends, and he's grown into being an important member of his community. From babysitting one another's dogs to having backyard barbeques to putting on holiday parties to being there to help a beloved pet pass over, John has found support (and gives support) in a way he didn't even know existed until Koda ran across the street. John didn't know that part of his healing process from his breakup was going to be that he had to learn to open his heart again. How smart is Koda to tap into this and teach him how to receive unconditional love, not just from Koda but from those surrounding him as well!

Through what he learned about the unconditional love of animals, John was so moved that he began donating his time to shelters. He's volunteered as a veterinary technician, and he continues to offer his moving mediumship demonstrations, from which he donates the proceeds to his animal charity organization.

Bringing Koda into his life helped John reopen his heart to others and find support in the world. He certainly hadn't planned on this, but Koda had a mind of his own and an animal lesson to teach John! What a little smartie he was! John had thought this little guy would meld right into his life. The reality was that John's life changed for the better in every area when he brought Koda into his life and listened to Koda's message.

Chapter Four

STEP 2:
DETERMINE THE LESSON

As you're very aware by now, the whole point of these human-animal relationships is to help the human involved learn a deep soul lesson. It's wonderful to know *how* the animal in your life is helping you learn, but it's very challenging to master the lesson if you don't know what it is.

Within each and every human-animal relationship lies a tutorial—something that, once you learn about it, will shift your life dramatically. This isn't an exaggeration in any way! Learning the lesson your animal is assisting you with will affect more than just your relationship with the animal—it will touch every aspect of your life. The possibilities for change are virtually endless once you get that lesson.

Three Facts about the Lesson

You've just finished figuring out how the animal in your life is working with you. This means you now have a solid handle on the methods this animal is using to draw your attention to the necessary places in your lives together that are being most affected by what you need to learn. Logically, it's now time to identify the lesson itself. Without knowing what you're supposed to be learning from all of this, you're simply identifying a challenge with your animal that you want to change, and that is something you probably already knew before you picked up this book!

There are three things to keep in mind as you begin looking for the lesson in this very special human-animal relationship:

1. Discovering the lesson presents a challenge for people used to busting their way through something to reach their goal. You can't *force* your identification of the lesson—it comes about through the development of a newfound understanding of yourself and your relationship with the animal. When you try to power through and make it happen (something that most people tend to do in their lives on a daily basis), you're not going to be able to go deep enough within to be effective. And that depth comes from the newfound understanding you're about to develop.

2. The second thing to keep in mind as you look for the lesson is that none of what you're experiencing with this animal is a coincidence. Animals don't affect us emotionally by accident. Every action they take is part of a great plan to stimulate us to evolve and learn. For some people, it may be challenging to accept this idea that there is more purpose and complexity to the animals in our lives than we've been taught to believe, but I'm willing to bet that if you're this far into this book, you've been able to recognize the truth in what I'm saying: animals are our teachers in every aspect of their being, from how they choose to behave, to how they make us feel, to how

they decide to act. To effectively uncover what lesson the animal in your life is helping you learn, remember there are no coincidences. That way, you'll have an easier time finding the meaning in every single thing that animal does.

3. When you finally do identify what the lesson is, it won't only benefit you in your relationship with this particular animal; it will also benefit you in every other area of your life. Picture that, through your parakeet, you've finally learned you are just as worthy of love as everyone around you. Imagine what a difference this would make in your life! You would alter your behavior in your friendships, you would have higher (and rightly so) expectations of those around you, and you would probably go a lot easier on yourself. If you're working on believing in your inner power through your work with your animal, you can bet that that newfound belief will alter how you run a meeting at work, how you approach your spouse, how you advance a project at school, and more. This is because the lesson centers on your deeply held beliefs about yourself, rather than on the specific actions you're taking. Yes, you read that right! The lesson is not about what you do but about why you do what you do (or feel what you feel) around your special animal. Your human-animal relationship isn't going to directly improve your teaching skills, but it very well could help you believe in yourself more, which in turn boosts your confidence, which helps you feel great as you're lecturing, which in turn helps you become a better teacher.

In a perfect world, where every human being is a fully functioning, healthy, productive member of a dynamic, happy, balanced society working in harmony with the earth, nature, the weather, and the universe, things would look very different from how they look today. All people would know, to the core of their being, that they are perfect, wonderful, protected, supported beings. They would align with unconditional love, and no one would view themselves as more valuable or more needy or less deserving or less smart or more vulnerable than anyone else.

Unfortunately, this isn't the way things are working in our world today. Through our experiences when we were young, many of us formed inaccurate and negative beliefs about ourselves, and these beliefs for most people have been the underlying dictator of our decisions since we first formed them many years ago. Identifying the lesson through your human-animal relationship helps you change these negative beliefs.

The Creation of Negative Beliefs

Although animals are working to help people develop positive beliefs about themselves, they aren't usually involved in the creation of people's negative beliefs. It's people who usually contribute to one another's negative beliefs about themselves. There aren't many people in our world who are truly aligned with unconditional love right now. It's something animals are looking to change, and it's why they are constantly working to help us align with our highest potential, living through unconditional love. No matter what negative belief the people and circumstances in our lives help us create, animals are there to assist in its release.

When you believe something negative about yourself, you have to learn the truth in order to change that belief. If you believe you are not lovable, for example, you have to learn that you are actually lovable in order to change that belief. If you believe you are a failure at whatever you do, you have to learn and believe that you actually can be successful in order to change that belief.

This means that to identify the lesson your animal is helping you learn, you must first identify the negative belief driving it.

Most of our negative beliefs about ourselves (such as "I'm not good enough," "I'm not lovable," or "I'm not safe") are created through our experiences with other people at a young age. Perhaps someone didn't get the type of love they needed, maybe a boy was left to fend for himself too often, or perhaps a young girl experienced a violation that made her feel unsafe in the world. Whatever the circumstances were, a negative belief was formed through that experience, and whatever that negative belief was, it will continue to affect the person into adulthood until it is understood and reversed. This is what animals are helping us do— realize the good within us and let go of all those negative beliefs!

We all place ourselves in the world based on what we believe about ourselves. Whether our beliefs are true or untrue, they simply dictate the choices we make in life. When you go through life believing that you're safe, awesome, wonderful, supported by the world around you, valuable, loved, worthy, and more, the decisions you make will reflect that. If you formed negative beliefs about yourself early on (when most people have), you've then fallen unknowingly victim to those negative beliefs as your guide to making the (often bad) choices you make today. Negative self-beliefs are like a slow-growing black mold, expanding their reach until they have overtaken every aspect of your life. The challenge is that this spreading occurs at such a young age that you don't detect it and at such a slow pace that it seems normal. When something changes bit by bit, it's hard to challenge it, because it's only a little different from what was happening before. This is how your negative beliefs came to have a hold on you, and your animal is helping you to bring these negative beliefs to the light.

If hidden within you is the belief that you aren't up to par with those around you, every decision you make is going to be based on proving that you *are* up to par or possibly based on proving that you're better than up to par. If your negative belief is that no one will ever come through for you, the actions you take will be to ensure that that doesn't happen. Perhaps you'll decide it's not okay to rely on others, and you subsequently have a difficult time asking for help. Every negative belief you have about yourself pulls you more deeply into survival mode and further and further away from aligning with the unconditional love of the universe.

When a man robs the apartment across the street to pay his rent because he believes that's his only option, he's in survival mode. For him, the end justified the means. Survival mode is the emotional space where many people spend most of their lives, doing whatever is necessary to cover up whatever negative belief they have about themselves, and it is exactly the mode of operation that will be most affected as you change and grow through the work in your human-animal relationship. When our animals present challenges to us, many of us go into survival mode, but when we work consciously with the animal, we'll encounter the opportunity to move toward unconditional love and shift those negative beliefs.

Animals have mastered unconditional love. In their natural habitat they don't experience negative beliefs about themselves. In fact, when untouched by humans (who have all sorts of negative beliefs about themselves), animals live in perfection. They wake every day believing in themselves. They accept without judgment that their limitations are not weaknesses they should be beating themselves up about but simply things that don't work for them. They adapt with their environment, and they accept their lives for what they are without spending time and energy in anxiety wondering and worrying about the past or the future.

Even the squirrel, gathering nuts for the winter, understands this as he goes about his daily routine with determination but without anxiety for what is coming.

People, on the other hand, do not usually operate this way. We worry about the future, our bank accounts, whether or not we offended that person at the office, what our life purpose is, whether our weight is appropriate, what other people think about us, and more. We tend to evaluate everything, and that evaluation often creates experiences that match what we're worrying about. Many people have lost touch with the part of themselves that connects to the unconditional love within, and it is the animals that are bringing us back in touch with it. They're helping us learn to love ourselves, accept our strengths and challenges, believe that we have power, operate from our own places of inner-knowingness, and more. And they are doing it every day through these beautiful human-animal relationships.

Figuring out your negative beliefs and the subsequent lesson the animal in your life is teaching you will open the door to a depth of work that you've probably never done on yourself before. Animals are assisting us in letting go of endless negative beliefs—now it's up to you to figure out what yours is.

How to Identify the Lesson

When you're searching for the lesson in your human-animal relationship, what you're really doing is working with your animal to correct some form of a harmful belief. I've found that every negative belief can eventually be drilled down to one of the following:

- I'm not good enough.
- I'm not safe, supported, or protected.

• I'm not worthy or deserving.

• I'm not lovable.

The majority of our challenges in life come back to an erroneous belief in at least one of these four ideas around self-love. Worried you can't get that new job? You're probably struggling with a belief about being good enough. Concerned about money? You probably believe you're unsupported in the world and others won't come through for you. Feeling overwhelmed with love for your cat because you've never let anyone into your heart before like this? You're most likely working on believing in your lovability.

Think again about that sentence you wrote earlier about your relationship with your animal as you worked on creating your Animal Lesson Statement from this template:

· ·

_____ *(Animal name)*

is doing _____ *(how)*

to help me learn _____ *(what lesson)*

by making me feel _____ *(emotions)*

and therefore do _____ *(work-arounds)*.

· ·

Let's use the hypothetical example of David and a raccoon. David has been dealing with a raccoon that continues to break into his basement and destroy property there, no matter how many different methods for stopping the raccoon David has implemented. As a result, David has been feeling angry, frustrated, fearful, and helpless.

David's Animal Lesson Statement could read something like this:

. . . .

The raccoon keeps

breaking into the basement

and wreaking havoc on my life

to help me learn _____ *(what lesson).*

. . . .

The next piece of this puzzle is to simply think about *why* the thing that the animal is doing (for David it would be breaking into his basement and destroying things) affects you the way it does (for David that would be anger, frustration, and helplessness). Emotions, while they may seem to just appear, are based on our feelings, our observations, and most importantly our beliefs about ourselves. David could have been a person who would laugh it off when he found out the wily raccoon got into his basement once again, but he wasn't. In fact, every time it happened he was frustrated, angry, and overcome by helplessness and fear. Why was he feeling those particular emotions? Why didn't he laugh it off or maybe decide to finally clean up the basement to change the situation? What was the reason he reacted that particular way? When we figure out why David felt those particular emotions, that's our clue right into his negative belief about himself.

Whenever the raccoon got into the basement, David immediately felt like he was losing control over his life. Why was this his conclusion? It's simply a wild animal breaking into a seemingly safe space. Couldn't he have concluded that the raccoon was being driven by food? Or perhaps that the raccoon was a trickster or maybe that it was sick? There are so many other roads that David could have gone down in reacting to this situation, but he consistently felt helpless every time the animal broke into his basement.

David experienced that anger and frustration because his repeated attempts at controlling the situation weren't working. He also experienced helplessness because what he was doing was ineffective. Every time he tried to control the situation and that control didn't stick, David felt fearful and helpless. Why was it so important to David to be able to control the situation? What does it say about David when he can't control that situation?

I bet you're beginning to clue in to David's underlying negative belief about himself. When the raccoon breaks in, David's first inclination is to control it, and when he can't control it, it elicits in him a feeling of not being good enough. This means that David's lesson through this raccoon is simply to learn that he is good enough (the opposite of his negative belief). But David's intellectual understanding, that he needs to learn that he's actually good enough, will not be a big enough realization. Through the raccoon, David is also going to have to believe this himself as well.

David's Animal Lesson Statement would now be this:

· ·

The raccoon keeps *breaking into the basement*
and wreaking havoc on my life to help me learn
that I am awesome, wonderful, and terrific.

· ·

You might be wondering how breaking into the basement could possibly be an effective way for any animal to teach someone about believing in themselves, and we will address that in a little bit. First, it's time for you to apply this to your own human-animal relationship. Luckily, with all the foundational work you've already done, this will be easy!

Think about the repeating pattern that the animal is experiencing with you, and take into account your circled emotions from chapter 3. Why does that repeating pattern make you feel those particular emotions? Would someone else feel a different way? Why do you always feel that way when this occurs? Look at how you're feeling and notice that, to some degree, it will match up with one of the four base negative beliefs. When you can correlate which negative belief is coming up in this situation with your animal, you have figured out the lesson. If you get stuck, simply go through that list of four negative beliefs and try out each one to see if it fits. At least one of those negative beliefs will fit the situation with your animal.

Once you've found one (or possibly more) of the four negative beliefs that are linked to the experience with your animal, stop for a moment. It's important to double-check that you've really nailed that lesson down as completely as possible.

First, ask yourself if this negative belief (or these negative beliefs) show up elsewhere in your life as well. For example, if one of the emotions you had around your horse was "powerless," do you feel powerless at home or at work too? If one of the negative beliefs you felt around your horse was "I'm not good enough," observe whether that belief rears up in other areas of your life as well. If your answer is yes, then you've hit the nail on the head, as the deep soul lessons that our animals are helping us learn are not limited to only our relationship with the animal.

If your answer is that no, you don't see this belief pattern occurring in other areas of your life too, then I urge you to continue with this process anyway using the belief you have uncovered. Often in my private practice, the belief is so deeply imbedded that my client doesn't see it outside of her human-animal relationship until later. This is not a bad thing or a good thing—it simply means you're in the very beginning stages of developing this awareness of yourself. You can be certain, though, that as you get further into this relationship with your animal, you'll start seeing it elsewhere in your day-to-day activities too!

If you've realized that you are learning several lessons through your animal, that's just fine, and that's very common. I always laugh when my private clients come to this point in the process and say things like, "Wow! Bernie is helping me learn three lessons!" I like to make the joke, "Well, then you must be really messed up!" But that's only a joke (and probably something that only I find funny). Discovering that your animal is assisting you in changing more than one belief only means that you're *really* ready to do this work. Additionally, the more you find to work with, the easier the whole process is, so be excited that your animal is assisting you in such an all-encompassing way! Those of you who are coming up with two or three different beliefs really should feel good about working with all of them in this process. Multitasking can be you and your animal's friend!

Take a moment to write out your Animal Lesson Statement here, as you have now determined it to be, and then you're ready to move forward.

. . . .

_____ *(Animal name)*

is doing _____ *(how)*

to help me learn _____ *(what lesson)*

by making me feel _____ *(emotions)*

and therefore do _____ *(work-arounds).*

. . . .

But wait! Your first instinct, at this point, will probably be to start working on changing the situation that is creating this challenge with your animal (so you can just "get through" this lesson), but it's not yet time. These human-animal relationships don't function in the same way that tackling a project at work does. Hold off just a little longer to learn the very best way to address this special relationship.

Animals in Action: Melanie and Squeak

When I first met Melanie Reynolds, she was an intense woman with some workaholic tendencies. I immediately liked her, as I have struggled with my own workaholic traits and have, in my years working with people and their animals, witnessed numerous variations of workaholism in people's lives.

In the human-animal work that Melanie and I were going to do together, she needed to choose one of her pets to be her guide. Immediately, Melanie knew that she wanted to choose her cat Sam. I asked her about Sam, and she said he was definitely the right choice because she felt that they really understood each other and that since things were going along pretty smoothly in their relationship at the time, he would be the best one to work with. Then she paused and said, "And that's good, because I really don't understand my other cat, Squeak, at all."

And right then, I knew that she just *had* to do her work with Squeak.

Melanie felt confused about Squeak and didn't know what to do with her or how to make her happy. Every day when she came home from work, she would drop her workbag on the table and immediately begin cooking dinner for herself and her husband. And every day, throughout the entire cooking process, Squeak would jump up on the table, the countertops, and anywhere else she could reach within the kitchen—all the while making the loudest unceasing meowing. If it took Melanie an hour to cook dinner, then Squeak followed her around for an hour, meowing the whole time.

When Melanie began to look more closely at her relationship with this very vocal cat, she noticed that Squeak meowed more loudly the days she was more frantic about getting dinner ready. She found this curious and decided to keep a closer eye on the situation to determine if it could yield any more information. Sure enough, after just a couple days of observation, she realized that the more she did in the evenings and the busier she was, the more annoying and loud Squeak became. Melanie remembered that an animal will keep sending a message, and that message will get louder and louder until you finally listen, and so she decided to listen.

Melanie determined that her emotional state of chaos when she came home from work was what Squeak was drawing her attention to, so she wanted to do something to shift that state. She started by working on simple energy management. Before walking up the stairs to her home after work each evening she would do one or two exercises to calm and center herself. By the time she reached the top of the stairs and opened the door to the kitchen, her whole demeanor would shift. Instead of throwing her workbag on the table and immediately beginning dinner, she would put her workbag away in its proper spot in the closet, spend a moment saying hello to Squeak and Sam, and only then would she begin the cooking process.

The result was an immediate change in Squeak. Instead of meowing at her, he laid about on the floor of the kitchen, lounging around while Melanie prepared the meal! After a few days of experiencing this each evening with Squeak, Melanie noticed something else: she was enjoying her evenings. She was moving through the night more deliberately, more slowly, and more peacefully, and it was making her feel a whole lot happier to be home. And with each passing moment that she felt happier, she also began to let go of many of the "have tos" that were driving her each night.

Before, Melanie was cooking dinner for herself and her husband, cleaning up dinner, doing the laundry, cleaning the house, and more into her evening. With her newfound peace, she started to relax about these things. The laundry *will* get done, she would think to herself, just perhaps not tonight, so she could have a little downtime before bed. Not doing it didn't mean she was shirking her duties or being a bad person. The dishes *will* get cleaned, but it wasn't the end of the world nor would anyone judge her if she didn't do them until the next morning.

Soon, Melanie found that she wanted to repeat her success at feeling peaceful at home at her work. She would take breaks throughout the day anytime she noticed that she was losing that wonderful sense of calm she felt. She also began measuring how much work she took on against how it would affect her ability to feel calm and peaceful, and it became easier to delegate and say no.

At her home things changed even more! When she came home one day in her new, more peaceful mood (and with a calm and quiet Squeak waiting by the door), her husband nonchalantly said, "Oh, Melanie, I did the laundry today." Melanie was floored. Her husband never did the laundry until she specifically asked him!

As Melanie continued to consciously manage her energy and emotions and let go of her need to do everything perfectly, Squeak continued to monitor her, keeping her in line whenever she fell off the wagon. Squeak had no problem meowing for an hour if Melanie forgot to take care of herself or tried to start proving her worth again through chores and tasks.

Recently, Melanie and I reconnected, and she told me about the new way Squeak had decided to ensure that she was taking care of herself—through a game of chase. Each night, prior to dinner, Squeak would run into the room where Melanie sat and skitter to a stop. She would meow once, look at her, and then run away, initiating a game of chase. Melanie would chase him all the way down the stairs where he would be waiting on her yoga mat, stretching and yawning. She wouldn't end the game until she got on her yoga mat and started stretching too.

It's pretty incredible what these animals do for us when we listen, isn't it?

Chapter Five

STEP 3:
FIND YOUR
WORK-AROUNDS

There is nothing more powerful than knowledge—once you have it, you realize you have choices. As a child of the '80s, I grew up watching those public service announcement TV spots in which drugs, bullying, feeling good about yourself, and other teen issues were addressed. At the end of each little short, a voice could be heard saying, "The more you know." The assumption was that if these public service announcements could educate kids about the best way to handle challenges by interspersing these *The More You Know* commercials in with the *The Incredible Hulk*, *The A-Team*, *Super Friends*, and whatever else the kids were watching, it would provide a needed leg to stand on for better informed decisions.

It's the same way with the animal in your life. He or she has been doing everything in her or his power to get your attention so that you can know and use that knowledge to make better decisions yourself. The difference between watching a PSA in the '80s and bonding in this way with your very special animal is that you get to play a more active role in the knowing. Yes, your animal is and has been showing you where to look, but now, it's time to start really looking! Fortunately, this simply requires you to "look" using a skill you've already innately possessed for your entire life. But first you must understand what you're looking at.

For most of your life, if not all your life, you've followed particular behavior patterns. As we begin to dissect those patterns, you're going to see that they are really just methods you've developed in order to avoid experiencing your negative beliefs. Perhaps when someone yells at you, you shrink away, or maybe you're someone who yells back. When a friend has a success, you may immediately congratulate them while secretly feeling jealous, or maybe you're someone who voices your jealousy as a joke while also patting your friend genuinely on the back. When you experience a pattern like this in your life, it's called a work-around.

Most people fall prey to their work-arounds because they don't realize they have a choice. You *can* change your work-arounds; it simply takes self-awareness. However, most of us avoid this completely, instead believing our work-arounds to be an integral part of our personality. It's easier to decide never to speak up (work-around) or to have to always beat everyone else at their game (work-around) than it is to slow down and take the time to understand what is really going on. It's easier to think that you're a competitive person (work-around) or that you always prefer to be alone (work-around) rather than talk to other people than it is to stop and look at what is really going on. And what is really going on is you have developed certain behavior patterns in order to avoid experiencing any of your negative beliefs.

You've already figured out the actions your animal is taking to help you and what lesson your animal is helping you learn.

You've also discovered which negative beliefs you and your animal are working on shifting within you. But there is another influence at play here: you also have to take into account the fact that you've had years to find ways to avoid experiencing those negative beliefs through your work-arounds. People avoid their negative beliefs by simply choosing to be unaware, reacting to life like robots programmed to behave in particular ways, and these are exactly the type of experiences your animals are helping you leave behind. If you're going to make changes within and learn that lesson the animal in your life is teaching you, you're going to have to stop choosing unawareness, stop choosing to let your work-arounds be your guide, stop letting your work-arounds dictate your personality, and instead start paying attention.

You're unaware when you unthinkingly perform the same action again and again without looking at what is driving that negative experience. You're unaware when you experience the same negative thoughts about yourself over and over, but you don't seek out why this is happening. People who go through life in this way often never come to realize that it is their work-arounds that are creating these situations for them, not their reality. And it's that lack of awareness that animals are here to shed a light on, exposing you to the places in your life where your thoughts and actions are holding you back and preventing you from becoming the very best person you can be.

Here are a few examples of work-arounds in action to get you starting to tune in to what your own work-arounds with your animal may be. I've also included potential reasons for those work-arounds, which are the negative beliefs that created the work-arounds in the first place.

- Overgiving to others in order to prove how good you are
- Overgiving at such a high clip that there is no space left within you to receive from others, thereby avoiding disappointment when you are not supported
- Being loyal to such a degree that it doesn't benefit you anymore, but it proves what a good, worthy, deserving, lovable person you are
- Flying under the radar so that no one notices you and makes you feel unsafe
- Flying under the radar so that no one can find you to support you, so you avoid disappointment
- Flying under the radar so that no one can get to know you and see that you're really not worthy, deserving, good enough, or loveable
- Sacrificing your own needs to prove you're a lovable person
- Being the aggressor in most situations to avoid disappointment when no one comes through for you
- Struggling to find your passion because you don't feel deserving of it
- Isolating yourself because you don't feel worthy of the love of others
- Isolating yourself because you don't feel good enough to be around others

And this is just the beginning! Clearly there are many, many different ways that people can create work-arounds for themselves, and this list doesn't even scratch the surface. It could be very challenging to figure out what your work-arounds are except that you have a secret weapon: your human-animal relationship. Your animal is working with you in exactly the area where your biggest work-arounds are causing pain and challenge, which means you've already begun laying the groundwork to start figuring yours out easily and smoothly by spending time coming to understand your relationship with your animal.

The key to discovering these work-arounds within your negative beliefs is to become innately curious in the relationship with your animal by developing a deep awareness of yourself and how you function within that relationship. As you become more and more curious, what you're really doing is delving further into what is actually occurring within you. Through curiosity with your animal, you'll start to break through the system you've had in place for many years that was designed to protect you from experiencing your negative beliefs about yourself.

Let's say you're forty years old and for as long as you can remember you have secretly questioned your lovability, which means that for almost forty years your decisions have been quietly directed by your desire never to experience feeling unlovable. Perhaps you've figured out that the more you love others, the more lovable you "look" (work-around); maybe you have determined that since no one is going to love you, it's easier to not love anyone either (work-around); or perhaps you believe that people cannot be trusted with your heart, so you have only surrounded yourself with animals (work-around). These work-arounds have become ingrained and a substantial part of who you are and have helped you mostly avoid feeling unlovable, as long as you can carry them out successfully.

When I first tried out meditating many years ago, I quit pretty quickly. The whole idea behind meditation is to calm the mind, basically creating a blue sky in your head, which will allow you to feel peaceful, reduce anxiety, and feel happier. When I noticed that my thoughts were wandering, I was to simply note this and come back to imagining this blue sky. The problem was that when I noticed that my mind had drifted, rather than just pulling myself back to the blue sky imagery, I wanted to notice what I had drifted toward, what kind of thought it was, and if it was the same kind of thought as last time. Did it make me feel good or bad? Was it a valid thought? What was I thinking about? Why was I thinking that? There was so much to know around that drifting away, that I began to feel that meditation didn't work on my brain.

But what did work on my brain was slowing down to examine what was going on with me, in my head, in my emotions, and in my heart during that meditation—and that's how curiosity with your animal works as well. My curiosity around which thought it was, if it was a pattern, and why it happened at that time actually allowed me to become more aware of what was going on with me. Years later, when I tried meditation again, I was much better at it because I had mastered the art of simply noticing my thoughts, actions, and emotions rather than critiquing them. Curiosity with your animal uses exactly the same process of understanding without judgment to just check out what is going on, why it's going on, and what's underneath it all.

Being curious with your animal allows you to start calling out all the thought processes that have resulted in those crazy work-arounds. Through curiosity, you naturally end up acknowledging that those thoughts, beliefs, emotions, feelings, and actions *do* exist. Let's use the example of Caesar the ferret making Luke feel that he wasn't good enough. Normally, Luke would simply work harder at hiding wires and ferret-proofing his house to what many would consider a somewhat insane degree (work-around) in order to prove to himself that he wasn't a bad ferret owner (negative belief). This method means that for Caesar's human to feel good enough, Caesar must not get into any trouble at any time in his life. In other words, Luke's feelings about himself have become dependent on his ferret! The point of this work with your animal, on the other hand, is to use curiosity to cull out the places in which these negative beliefs, feelings, and work-arounds exist so that they can be naturally shifted. In this case it would be to discover what Luke's beliefs about himself were and how they were being controlled by his ferret.

Finding Your Work-Arounds through Curiosity

Through their deep work with us, animals are demanding an end to this lack of awareness in the human population, an end to our mindless work-arounds that enable us to avoid understanding and releasing our painful beliefs within, an end to our justification of the hurt we put on others, both human and animal, in the name of survival. Luckily, the animal that has stolen your heart has been quietly (and sometimes not so quietly) cultivating your relationship together to specifically assist you in addressing your lack of understanding of yourself.

In order to take advantage of everything the animal in your life has to offer you, you'll simply begin to uncover your personal work-arounds. This means becoming mindful of your feelings, thoughts, actions, reactions, and body and no longer accepting these things that you have no control over as "the way things are." And you're going to do this using a skill most people perfected at an early age: curiosity.

Yes, discovering your work-arounds through your animal really is as easy as becoming curious about yourself and your relationship with your animal. Curiosity is simple. It isn't daunting—it's just getting to know something a little better. It's going to help you greatly in this special relationship and beyond. After all, how can you grow, learn, or make changes if you have no idea when you're doing something to avoid feeling something? If you don't pay attention to how you're feeling, you can't learn about your feelings, and you simply aren't opening the door to a deeper understanding of yourself that allows for growth and change.

Recently, I was speaking with a former student about the curiosity part of the process with the animal. She told me that it was hard to recall what that learning process felt like because now that she's through it, living with curiosity just seems so natural. She laughed as she said, "It's challenging to even remember when I wasn't aware of myself like this!"

Think back to that beautiful statement you've written about the relationship between you and your animal and the negative beliefs your animal is assisting you in changing—"I'm not good enough," "I'm not safe/supported/protected," "I'm not deserving/worthy," or "I'm not loveable." We spend our lives trying to avoid things that we don't like, feelings we don't enjoy, people who make us feel bad, and situations that hurt us. The truth is that, at the very deepest levels of our being, we do everything we can to avoid any ickiness in our lives. But what would happen if, instead of avoiding the upset, you explored that feeling? Would it get worse? Would it get better?

When you're attached to something, the loss of it is always much greater than if you didn't care, even if the outcome is the same. When you're unattached to something, it's easier to get the big picture because none of your emotions or fears are getting in the way to drive you in certain directions. When you're out in your field behind the barn thinking up fun things to train your horse to do, you're probably going to have a much better day than if you are trying to cram in as many horse tricks as possible in order to prove to your boss that you really are a great horse trainer.

You're in a more neutral place and are free to move through the experience as you're moved to when you're working with your horse because you love him and feel moved by him. When the two of you are together in that field, it feels like a beautiful connection overcomes the two of you. There is no need to prove or disprove, protect or promote in that moment with your horse; you are purely there for the experience. When you are working with the horse to prove you can do something, to show someone else that you can do it, to show that you're better than someone else, or to prove you're worth the money, you're now placing your value on what you are able to achieve, which means that the only way to come out of the experience feeling good is to meet or, more likely, exceed your goal. You are no longer unbiased, you have become attached to the outcome, and that outcome is what tells you your worth.

Through curiosity, you can do that training for your boss without the results having anything to do with your value or worth. When you become curious about yourself, your feelings, your emotions, your physical sensations, your drives, and your thoughts, you can actually release that attachment and perform better than you ever have before! Curiosity requires you to do the exact opposite of what most people have been doing for their entire life: instead of running away from the icky feelings by living on autopilot, curiosity will force you to take note and understand what's really going on. For years you've done everything in your power not to notice your discomfort. Now, with your animal supporting you all the way, things are about to change in the biggest way possible.

The challenge then becomes this: How do you become curious with yourself? I mean, you've been hanging out with yourself for your entire life. How do you now try to look at yourself through this new lens and see something different from what you've been seeing for the past thirty, forty, fifty, sixty years? Because curiosity is just an intense desire to know or understand, starting this process is actually very easy. Whenever you're around your animal, merely start paying attention to the emotions that come up. That's it!

Practicing curiosity with your animal is very straightforward. For those of you who are working with an animal that you have easy access to, such as a dog or cat that lives in your home, just start noticing how you feel when you're interacting with that animal and what kinds of things you do as a result of those feelings. For those of you who are working with an animal you don't see every day—this could be Lucy the cow from the farm next door or the abused elephant in India you recently read about on social media—you'll concentrate more on the feelings and emotions that come up when you think about this animal or read about this animal and what you do as a result. Either way, the curiosity is about starting to notice what is going on within you when you interact with your animal. While this may seem obvious at first (you may be thinking to yourself, "Well, of course I'm frustrated and decide to shut down when she keeps doing that over and over again!"), there's a lot more to curiosity than first meets the eye.

The nature of curiosity is 100 percent neutral. Scientists are curious as they try to understand why something happens. Children are curious when presented with a new task, such as putting a block set together. Cats are curious when presented with a new experience, like tasting a new food or exploring a new sound. The thing about curiosity is that there is no judgment and no expectation. When the curious scientist tests her hypothesis and it turns out to be incorrect, she simply adjusts her hypothesis. When the child accidentally knocks the new block set over, he might cry for a moment (as he's just a child), but then he'll set about putting the blocks back together. When the cat hears the new sound, he sets off to check it out. Maybe he finds the source and takes a swipe at it. Perhaps he attacks it. Whatever he does, he wants to figure out what is going on.

And that's what I'm asking you to do when you're with your animal: simply be inquisitive about what is happening with you on a mental, emotional, physical, and spiritual level. Think of yourself as that cat checking out that weird sound and just notice. How do you feel in this moment as you witness your parrot pulling out all his feathers? Are you experiencing an emotion? What are your thoughts? Do you feel anything going on in your body? Is that negative belief you identified earlier at play? Does the pulling of the feather create a negative emotion? Were you thinking something negative beforehand? Does watching this occur make you want to take some action?

The more curious you are and the more you step outside of yourself and observe as you go through an experience with your animal, the less charged your thoughts and feelings will naturally become and the less need you'll have to do one of your work-arounds. Rather than running away from or ignoring that tough moment with your animal, stepping into it with curiosity again and again will actually assist you in understanding yourself better and defusing the situation. It will subsequently mean the work-arounds that you used to do as a result of the feelings and emotions you were trying to avoid become less and less necessary.

You can do a lot with this whole curiosity thing. When your curiosity enables you to observe that you're experiencing one of the emotions you identified earlier in the book, it's actually a signal to become even more curious. Take note of that emotion:

"I'm noticing that I now feel embarrassed by Caesar's behavior." Then link it up to the underlying belief the animal is helping you change: "I notice that I'm now feeling embarrassed because it makes me seem like I'm terrible at taking care of my ferret, which activates my belief that I'm not good enough." Curiosity really can be this easy if only you make the effort to do it.

Third-Person Method

One way to embrace this curiosity around your relationship with your animal is to start observing it in more of a third-person mode. In the first-person perspective, we talk about ourselves as "I"—"I notice that every time Caesar does this, I feel frustrated, and I find myself closing off to him." But if you're struggling to see the pattern through your curiosity, it may work to talk about yourself, to yourself, in the third person. Certainly, this is not a normal way to behave (I definitely want to giggle when people in real life start talking about themselves in the third person!), but for many, it is key to being able to fully take note of what is happening.

In the first-person perspective, you are saying this: "Every time Caesar does this, I feel frustrated." Instead, in the third-person perspective, you are saying this: "Every time Caesar does this, Luke looks frustrated and upset. In fact, he looks a little bit hurt, and then it seems that he closes himself off from Caesar, his ferret, turning his back and walking away." Using the third-person perspective is a bit like telling a story, but that story is about yourself. This may allow you to notice things about you and your animal that you might otherwise overlook because you are so involved in the situation. Throughout their lives, most people have tried *not* to be curious about themselves. Be prepared for it to take a little effort for you to become a curiosity expert in discovering all the places your animal is pushing you, and use whatever method necessary to effectively become the master of curiosity about you and your animal.

Memory Method

As you improve at being curious when you're with your animal, the things that you choose to get curious about with your animal will change. If I were to ask Luke to give me examples of times when he experienced an emotional thought of not being good enough around Caesar, he surely could, and it wouldn't take him being an expert at curiosity to do so. He'd remember the many times his negative belief arose in his relationship with Caesar, and he'd be able to account for them almost effortlessly. Memory is your curiosity starting point with your animal.

Consider for a moment your relationship with your animal. Think back to the numerous times your experience with your animal elicited the particular negative beliefs, emotions, and thoughts about yourself that you've identified here. Choose just one of those memories and think about it now as if you were watching it on TV, only you don't know what the show is about: "Oh, when he chewed the electrical cord, my immediate thought was that I did something wrong. I noticed this made me feel bad about myself, and I didn't want to hang out with him anymore. Oh yeah! And then I remember thinking to myself, 'Of course I have a ferret that misbehaves—it's all I deserve!'" Just follow the course of the interaction from a detached place. No judgment, no criticism—just notice what happened emotionally, physically, mentally, and spiritually. Observe your memory and feel excited with each piece you can witness, and tie it back to the negative beliefs and thoughts your animal is helping you master.

When you're recalling a memory, it's pretty easy to become curious about it and link what you're observing in the memory to the work that your animal is doing with you. Being in a state of curiosity about the past, which allows you to become objective, much like talking about yourself in the third person can do, allows you to look and learn rather than be bowled over by the memory. It's also a great way to practice detached curiosity, since the next goal is to be able to practice it *while* the interaction with you and your animal is taking place rather than in hindsight.

Helpful Hints

Simple, real-time curiosity can be a bit more challenging to perform than memory curiosity at first. When you're curious about an experience you had in the past, two things happen. First, you feel as if you almost have more control over it because you can choose to remember it however you want, and, second, because the experience happened in the past, there is a natural access to more objectivity around it. This gives you the power to parse it out for your curiosity exercise. Real-time curiosity with your animal doesn't allow for any cherry-picking because you are *in* the experience, but the more you practice it, the easier it becomes. At first, when you're in the moment with your animal, your natural tendency is going to be to want to judge rather than observe, but a gentle reminder that you're doing a curiosity experiment on yourself should allow part of you to be able to step back and begin witnessing what is transpiring between you and your animal.

The more often you can become curious around your animal, the better you'll become at this whole curiosity thing—and the less you'll find yourself attached to your behaviors and subsequent emotions with your animal. Curiosity is helping you grow your awareness of yourself, the drives behind your behavior, what your behavior really is, and where it's coming from. Let me repeat that: the more you practice curiosity with your animal, the less of a hold your behavior, thoughts, feelings, and emotions have over you (i.e., your work-arounds), and the more you create space for change within you and for an upgraded relationship to emerge between the two of you.

Curiosity is a funny thing. The more curious you are, the more things there are to be curious about and the less seemingly important the things you're curious about become. Instead of practicing curiosity around that time you felt devastated by that hawk that swooped down and tried to take your little dog for dinner, forcing you to feel unsafe in your backyard for the next two years, you're more curious about the time that your dog nudged the cup on the coffee table so that it tipped over. Your curiosity is changing because you're starting to solve the mystery behind your emotions, negative feelings, and actions (your work-arounds) for the big, obvious events in your relationship with your animal, so the smaller moments are the ones that start to stand out. It's like you have solved the mystery of the big stuff, and so you start fine-tuning your curiosity to those experiences that you have yet to understand, those that may have gone under the radar and unnoticed by you previously.

Isn't it interesting that once you start to realize why your dog makes you feel not good enough, why you can't say no to your horse, what drives you to hate your neighbor's dog, or why the squirrels in the backyard make you feel scared and unsafe, that those things lose some of their charge with you? When you finally see how your rooster's ability to escape every enclosure is linked to your feelings of never being safe, your thoughts, feelings, and actions start to slowly change. As your interest is piqued, you begin seeking out more places where this dynamic is playing out that you may never have noticed before. A few weeks ago the bear could have walked up to your dining room window and looked in and you wouldn't have noticed how unsupported that made you feel because all you could concentrate on being curious about was the fact that the bear kept breaking into your garage and you couldn't find a way to keep him out. As you hone your curiosity skills, your ability to connect this smaller moment to that negative belief you hold within you is becoming honed as well.

The ultimate goal in being in this state of curiosity with your animal is to keep honing your skills until you can uncover and observe those negative thoughts about yourself in formerly unexpected moments with her. The more you use curiosity to observe the relationship between you and your animal, the more you are breaking apart that system of unconsciousness that was so heavily embedded within you, preventing you from experiencing the full potential of your human-animal relationship.

The challenge, as you become more and more curious, will be not to resist it and, more importantly, not to try to control it or make yourself make changes because of it. Being curious means you're *really* looking at yourself, and there is a very human part of all of us that is going to want to observe, figure it all out, and then change our behavior immediately. I've seen it time and time again with my students and private clients: their curiosity has shown them the light around their beliefs, feelings, and behavior, and because they finally appreciate how these things are no longer serving them, they decide to start doing the opposite of their work-arounds.

And that kind of makes sense, right? You finally see how your beliefs and behavior are affecting every day of your life with your animal, and you don't want that to happen anymore, so you decide to change it. Perhaps you've been overloving your cat, you've resisted training your dog, or you've been afraid to let the new pig meet the old pigs because of your negative beliefs. What's the first thing you can do to alter those beliefs and behaviors? Let the pigs meet each other, right? No. In fact, using willpower in this way would actually impede you from learning everything you can from working with your animal. Simply doing the opposite of your work-around or telling yourself you shouldn't be feeling this way anymore will not even come close to accomplishing the deep, internal growth that you can achieve through this work with your animal. Don't fall into this trap.

Let's say you never feel safe or protected in the world (your negative belief), and as a result, you never ride your somewhat unruly horse. Then, let's say you move into curiosity around this relationship and you realize how much you're missing out on with your horse, how you're even afraid to enter the barn, and how your horse is suffering because he's not getting enough exercise. Some people would try talking themselves into feeling safe: "It's just a horse, you can do this. People ride horses every day." But the minute you get on your horse, your fears—based on your deep-down belief that you're not safe—are going to pop up. And your horse is going to feel your fear and react. You're putting yourself in a position where you are in conflict with yourself and with what you believe. Not fun. Not easy. This work with your animal is about changing your negative beliefs into positive beliefs so that the things you want to do, achieve, and feel are effortless. Period. When beliefs change, your behavior naturally changes. It's that simple. For example, when you go from believing that you're unlovable and making choices based on that belief to believing in your lovability, everything about how you place yourself in the world changes along with it—not because you're telling yourself to change, but because it will naturally happen.

When your negative belief remains intact but you decide to act as if it doesn't exist by pushing yourself to do the "proper" thing, you're challenging yourself to rely on your willpower to change your life. And what does that mean? It means that you have to keep your eye on the ball of that change forever. The moment you let go of those reigns, your negative beliefs about yourself will regain control and start guiding your behavior again. You can't talk yourself into a different belief unless you want to keep talking yourself into it again and again and again. And that's a lot of work. That's more work than I want to put into anything. You actually have to change the belief within *first* before the behavior and work-arounds will ever change.

Let's say that by working with your animal so far, you've realized that you have a negative belief that you aren't lovable, and that is reflected in your relationship with your rescue horse Ticonderoga through her affection for you. Every time she gives you love and attention, you know you did the right thing in rescuing her and you feel like you're on track. Every time she gives you less attention than you think she should be giving you, you feel bad about yourself and question if you're doing enough to earn her love. In fact, when she doesn't give you attention, you even wonder if she doesn't like you, and it makes you feel guilty. Now that you know this about yourself, you feel like you've been putting too much pressure on Ticonderoga, and you feel like you have been messing this whole relationship up. As a result, you decide that you shouldn't be the one rehabilitating her and you hire someone else instead. When you see Ticonderoga, you try not to let your heart melt if she nuzzles you, and you try to not be attached to her at all because you don't want to base your goodness on whether or not she is well rehabilitated.

Does this seem like an effective way to learn about yourself? Does it seem like it is growing or assisting the relationship between you and Ticonderoga? Does it even feel good to try and censor your feelings for this horse you've just rescued? Does it feel like this relationship has a chance of progressing at all? The answers, as you've already noticed, are all no. In this instance, you're using willpower to try and create change rather than going within and working *with* your animal to change your beliefs about yourself and open your heart. Willpower is a conditional thing based on your determination, your force, and your ability to remain focused at all times. This doesn't seem very fun to me. Sure, I like to be focused, but I don't want things in my life to go downhill or return to a state I don't love just because I didn't maintain my focus 100 percent of the time.

Being curious with your animal should be just that: working in alignment with your animal. Curiosity is not an act that directly creates change; it is simply the act of observing objectively and learning from what you're noticing. Change indirectly results. It is not about altering the relationship between you and your animal. Yes, changes are going to come about because of this incredible work that you're doing, but they are not going to come about because you forced them to happen. They're going to arise through this new awareness of yourself, of your animal, and of the relationship that you have with her. Don't force this. Avoid pushing in any way. Just spend your time observing and getting to know your personal invisible system of negative beliefs about yourself that your animal is helping you become acquainted with.

One more thing about curiosity—have fun with it! If you can remember to laugh at yourself a little bit, it's going to make the process a whole lot more enjoyable, and it will prevent you from becoming critical of yourself, your thoughts, your emotions, and your actions. The more curious you are, the more your animal will throw you things to be curious about! I've seen many people struggle to be curious because they were taking it too seriously and looking too hard. You don't have to push here—just pretend that you are your own science project and that you're forming your hypothesis about the various situations with your animal. Your animal will help you find and, yes, create the perfect moments to observe and learn from. Just trust her and have fun with this!

Animals in Action: Anne and Kelly

I first met Anne Quick at an Animal Communication workshop I was teaching at the Kripalu Center in the Massachusetts Berkshires. She had a super cute haircut and her own unique dressing style, and because of her wide-eyed, deer-in-the-headlights look, she stood out to me within the group of twenty or so students. Anne is one of those people who is always smiling, and yet you can see the wheels behind her smile are always turning. I noticed there was a certain unrest in her smile, even as she worked with the other students to connect with the various class animals.

In my work, whether it's a weekend workshop, a one-hour class, or even an international retreat, I tend to attract very sensitive yet very analytical folks. I always laugh about this when starting a new class because I can look around and see everyone picking apart everything I say, everything anyone else does, and everything they do to the finest detail. Anne is one of those people.

During a break on the first day of our class, Anne approached me out in the hallway. I remember she looked a little worried and seemed unsure as she waited to talk with me.

"I don't think I can do this," she said as she nervously looked in all directions except at me.

Now, here's the funny thing. I like to think of myself as a kind person, one who helps her students get through the tough times, one who provides a supportive environment, and one who would never laugh at her students. But that's exactly what I did. I laughed. In fact, I laughed heartily.

"Of course you can! I just saw you do it!" I told her. And I had just seen her do it. She would present her impressions from our practice animal to the group, and she would talk as if she didn't know what she was doing and as if she were getting information that didn't apply (but it did). It wasn't just her cool hair or her funky style that made her stand out in the class to me, it was also her innate skill coupled with her lack of confidence, something I see again and again in my work.

And that was the beginning of a very cool relationship in which I would witness someone move from fearful and full of depression, self-doubt, insecurity, and anxiety, to confidence, a great sense of humor, and an ability to see the depth in others in a way that would allow her to assist people and their animals profoundly. Just because of who she finally realized she is.

But not yet. I didn't know it at the time, but Anne had just been in the hospital for depression and had chosen to come to my workshop to learn more about how to read animal body language in order to be a better owner to her two dogs. She didn't realize that animal communication involved the heart, intuition, being clear, and being sensitive. She got a huge surprise!

Later that year, Anne chose to start working on her relationship with her retired Greyhound, Kelly, and me through my Soul Contraction Certification with Animals program. Her relationship with Kelly had been challenging because Kelly was not affectionate toward her, and this was creating a lot of anxiety in her life. Kelly didn't like loud sounds, including the sounds of kicking a ball.

Anne lived right across the street from a school, so this was a problem. Additionally, every time Kelly shied away from Anne, Anne questioned whether she was the right rescuer for her and felt that she wasn't doing a good enough job. It was a tough situation for someone who had been struggling deeply with depression, anxiety, not believing in herself, and feeling separate and apart from the world.

Through her work with Kelly in my program, Anne realized that Kelly was helping her in two very important ways. First, Kelly was doing everything in her power to bring Anne's anxiety problem to the forefront by mirroring it back to Anne. With Kelly around, there was no way that Anne was going to be able to continue to ignore her anxiety, which had been her work-around until that time. Each time Kelly was anxious, Anne used curiosity to begin to look at herself, her thoughts and feelings, and what she was doing at the time. This curiosity brought to the forefront something that Anne had been pushing away for years: how dominantly anxiety had been ruling her life. The more aware she was of Kelly's anxiety and triggers, the more aware she became of her own, which started to make her feel that her own anxiety was somewhat pointless. It was a circular pattern for her that just kept going around because she had been letting it. Kelly was bringing awareness to that, so Anne could finally stop going in circles through simple understanding.

Kelly was also helping Anne address her inability to trust that others would love her as she would love them. Anne watched as Kelly shut herself off to experiences simply because Anne was allowing her past to drive her present. It brought an awareness of her own life to the forefront, and soon Anne was able to see this for herself in her day-to-day activities. Her curiosity started kicking in when she realized how much she was missing out by not trusting, and with Kelly by her side, they started exploring more of life together.

Through Kelly and Animal Lesson work, Anne shifted her beliefs about herself, and the most beautiful result was that Kelly did too! Today, Anne and Kelly have a beautiful relationship that is relatively anxiety free (unless Anne starts to waver, and then Kelly is right there reminding her). Anne's newfound love of herself has allowed her to open up to love with others as well, and she's now in a relationship with someone who values her for all that she brings to the table. And through all this work, Anne realized that she wants to help others evolve and grow just like she did. She's now pursuing her dream as a professional animal communicator, with Kelly right by her side, and she did, in fact, become my very first Certified Soul-Level Animal Communication Practitioner!

Chapter Six

STEP 4: THE DECISION-MAKING PROCESS

As you know now, animals are sentient beings that are exceptionally in tune with the needs, feelings, desires, emotions, and thoughts of humans. When you allow one into your life in any way, that animal taps in to you, whether you asked for it or not. In fact, you can't stop it! It doesn't matter if you're bringing a rescued dog into your home, carrying an injured squirrel to the vet, introducing a new cow into your herd, or sending money to help an animal on the other side of the world. That animal will still tap in to the deepest part of you, innately understand your challenges, and work in her way to help you master them. It's a beautiful process but one that is much more difficult for everyone involved if you don't know where she's helping you or that she's even trying to help you—hence your reading of this book.

Working your curiosity with your animal has assisted you in developing a newly heightened awareness of yourself, why you do the things you do, and why you feel the things you feel. You've not only identified what negative beliefs and work-arounds your animal is helping you to change but also how your animal is working to do this. The more curious you've been, the more you've observed your feelings, thoughts, and actions around your animal, which helps you better understand the self you've developed and better uncover those negative beliefs. (Good thing you had an animal to help you with this, right?)

As you learned in the last chapter through your curiosity, you've also proven to yourself the existence of your negative beliefs that have been unknowingly driving your choices, actions, decisions, and more with your animal. With each moment of observation in your relationship with your animal, it has become more and more clear that many (if not all) of the decisions you've been making are stemming from some belief of inadequacy within you. The beautiful part is that realizing this actually empowers you rather than crushes you; now that you can identify it, you can choose whether or not to use it.

Your belief that you are not worthy (or whatever your negative belief might be) is only a filter. By definition, a filter is something that you can change or remove, and that is what you're now prepped to be able to do. Becoming disinterested in the old negative beliefs you've been working with is just another way to look at removing the filter of that negative belief. Once you achieve this, you're finally free to decide your actions, behavior, thoughts, and feelings with your animal from a wonderful, calm, clear-headed positive belief about yourself, rather than through that old filter of negative belief. While this concept seems pretty easy, most people resist it. Because the filter is what we know, it's where we go; it's what we're interested in perpetuating. For many years that negative belief filter has been your comfort zone, and we all know how comfortable our comfort zone is, even when it isn't really! By working with your animal, you're beginning to expand and shift that comfort zone into a bigger, happier, more accepting comfort zone.

As you know, negative belief filters are most often developed through personal experiences early on in life. Perhaps you didn't receive the love or the protection you were looking for as a young girl. Perhaps you were always second fiddle in the hierarchy of the children in your family. Whatever the circumstances, things came together in a particular way to create a repeated experience that shaped your belief system about yourself. So to change your belief system, we have to do the same thing: create a repeated experience with your animal that will reinforce the new, positive belief you are looking to have and make the old belief seem outdated, unnecessary, and even just plain stupid. Doing this is simple, but it grows within you, rather than being forced through you.

It's surprisingly easy to begin transforming those negative beliefs you've discovered through your work with your animals. First, you use your newfound curiosity skills to notice that one of those challenging moments with your animal is about to occur. Once you've noticed that, and before the challenging moment actually occurs, you simply decide how you want to handle the situation and then you take that action. The more often you follow this process, the stronger the effect it has on helping you change those negative beliefs.

I realize this sounds as if it might just be too easy. People often don't believe that viewing their relationship with their animal in this way could actually produce change and growth and help them let go of their negative beliefs! This is why I have divided the process up—to help you see a structure in something that is a very natural process when you become truly curious within your human-animal relationship.

Notice That a Challenging Moment
Is about to Occur

As you advance in being curious about your relationship with your animal, your understanding of what is happening between you and your animal advances as well. This evolves innately as you continually observe yourself in this special relationship. You're on track to move from observing moments that happened in your memories (the past), to observing events and feelings occurring between you and your animal in the moment (the present), to finally being able to predict that a moment worth observing is *about* to happen (the future). Being able to predict when one of these particular moments with your animal is about to occur is one of the main goals of curiosity. Think of yourself as a fortune-teller in this relationship. Here's an example of what predicting one of those challenging moments with your animal looks like:

Before Charlie started witnessing and observing his relationship with a famous elephant on social media, he often felt overwhelmed by his love for this elephant. As he continued to be curious about this relationship, he eventually noticed that each time he thought of the elephant, he felt in awe of the fact that the elephant was so comfortable being his elephant-like self that everyone loved him for it. He also noticed that his overwhelming love for this elephant also made his feel inadequate, and he realized that when he read about this elephant, he himself would begin experiencing emotions of unworthiness. Soon, Charlie was able to predict this: "Oh, when I read a story on social media about another amazing feat this elephant has accomplished, I'm going to feel small." And this is what predictions look like in the human-animal relationship—simply knowing how you're going to feel or react in a certain situation. It isn't complicated or fancy. Predictions are just the knowing that in this particular place, event, or experience, a certain negative belief around your animal will show up. Charlie was able to uncover that his belief that he needed to do more to earn the love of others was being triggered through his relationship with this famous elephant.

Each time you enter into that situation with your animal, that negative belief filter will appear until you've shifted it. Start calling out various situations in your human-animal relationship where those emotions you uncovered earlier show up again and again. If you can't do this yet, it's okay. It just means that you have to spend a little more time being curious so that you can be sure you understand where this filter shows up and how it affects you within your human-animal relationship. Simply spend some more time (maybe another day or two) being fully present in your relationship with your animal until you get to the point where you can easily name five to ten places where that filter always appears. You'll want to have as many moments as you can in your pocket because the more moments in which you can predict what is about to happen with you and your animal, the easier it will be to allow this to grow and change. Don't rush it. Be patient and wait until you've reached the point where your pockets are symbolically overflowing, so you know you're really equipped to continue on this amazing journey with your animal. Don't you feel like it's finally time to stop living with that filter?

Decide How to
Handle the Situation and Take Action

The process you go through to decide how you want to handle the predicted situation between you and your animal has a truly significant effect on changing your belief, but probably in a different way than you think. Imagine that you're driving in your car on a crowded highway and a small red car cuts off the cars several lengths ahead of you, making one of the cars swerve into the next lane to avoid a collision. While watching this occur in front of you, how do you feel? You'll probably experience various things like anger, confusion, concern, fear, surprise, or frustration, for example. Now imagine that the cars in the offender's lane are all slowing down, while the cars in your lane are maintaining their speed. As a result you're going to end up right next to that offender's car, and you're going to have a choice to make. Now, if you were my husband, your emotions might compel you to bring your car even with the offender's car to give the driver a super angry look in hopes of teaching him about proper driving. If you were someone else, perhaps you would just ignore the offender or try to get away from the offender's car.

When we make choices while we are emotionally charged, those choices aren't necessarily the best choices in the long run. Let's say you're taking a walk on a new path through the forest with your dog. You're pretty calm on the walk, giving a few corrections here and there to your dog, who is also pretty calm, walking on the leash by your side. You reach a waterfall and as you're taking it in, you hear something in the bushes next to you. It sounds big. In a panic, you drop your dog's leash and go running back down the path, screaming, with your dog nowhere in sight. It takes several days to recover your dog, who ended up getting lost in the woods, and you find out later that the rustling in the bushes you heard was merely a family of wild turkeys that had taken up residence near the waterfall. Ugh.

Now let's look at this story from a different angle. You're on that new path with your dog, enjoying yourself. You've already heard stories from others about the wild turkey family that was living in the vicinity, particularly near the water, and you've decided that you would love to be able to see them. As you reach the waterfall, you know that if you're going to see them, this could be the place, so when you hear a rustling, instead of panicking, you're prepared. You think to yourself, "Could this be the wild turkeys? How do I want to handle this?" After a moment of being quiet, you think you see a baby wild turkey run by, so you decide to sit down with your dog and wait to see what happens. In less than five minutes, the entire wild turkey family emerges from the brush and starts walking down the trail. You're treated to a spectacular moment.

The decisions you make are very different depending on your emotional state. It's really hard to make solid, balanced, good decisions when you're emotionally activated (in this instance, panicked). Deciding how you want to handle a situation is all about making your decision from a place of calm, clarity, and balance rather than from fear, worry, and insecurity. Coincidentally, most people are not able to make their decisions from a balanced place within themselves, instead reacting to the feelings within, whether or not those feelings are balanced or justified.

It's all about timing. Making your decision *before* the challenging moment with your animal is about to occur not only takes advantage of the calmer mindset you're in, it also takes advantage of the time and space that is created by your prediction. Before the challenge moment with your animal arises, you're in your normal, everyday (and most likely calmer and easier) emotional state. Wouldn't this be a better, healthier place from which to make important decisions? Deciding how you're going to behave, how to understand a situation, and whether or not to take it personally is much easier when you're not in the thick of it, and it is predicting your challenging moment with your animal that allows you to do this.

When you predict that a challenging moment is about to show up, you are lengthening the time you have between when you have to decide on your behavior and when you actually need to take action on it. That's the luxury the curiosity creates—you're now able to see what is about to occur, what you are about to experience, and what your animal is about to do, rather than be washed over by the moment. Isn't it just wonderful to become so conscious?

Let's use the example of Ricardo and the squirrel and bird situation in his backyard. Ricardo has noticed that there is a bird that frequents his backyard, and this bird seems to have a problem with its foot. He doesn't know if the foot is deformed or broken or something else, but the moment he saw this, he wanted to help this bird the best he can. The problem is that there is an extremely large red squirrel that keeps chasing the deformed-footed bird away whenever she is at the feeder eating. The squirrel pops up (from seemingly nowhere), does that loud squirrel screech, and scares the poor bird away. Ricardo has noted that this is a challenging situation for him because every time it occurs, he feels like he should be doing more. He's upset that this bird might be experiencing pain and that he's not able to fix it, and his feelings of helplessness come out. As Ricardo continues the process, his curiosity allows him to see that his feelings of not being good enough are being activated through the squirrel and bird situation, and his work-around is to "fix" the bird to prove his own value and goodness.

Now that Ricardo understands his situation, he delves deeper. He's able to predict that whenever the bird lands on the bird feeder and that squirrel shows up, his negative belief filter is going to be highly activated. Luckily, this realization is a good thing! Ricardo now has *time* and *space* available to him because he is able to foresee that he and the bird are about to go through another one of those challenging experiences; he just put fresh food into the feeder, and the bird usually shows up to eat within a few minutes of that.

Ricardo can now take advantage of the time and space he's created by predicting the challenge moment with the bird. Since Ricardo's feelings of not being good enough have not yet been activated (the bird and squirrel have not yet shown up), he's in an emotionally clean and clear place from which to make his decision about how to handle the approaching situation. Normally, he couldn't do anything once the bird showed up because the squirrel quickly followed.

But here, Ricardo has a choice. Lots of choices, in fact.

Option 1: Ricardo can let everything progress as it usually does, with the deformed-footed bird showing up to feed on the new food in the birdfeeder and the squirrel chasing him away.

Option 2: Ricardo can think about these animals in the past and remember that only the squirrel is scared of him. Through this clarity, Ricardo can decide to sit in a chair in the backyard in order to scare the squirrel away but allow the bird to get to the feeder.

Option 3: Ricardo can ask his friend to build a squirrel feeder so the squirrel no longer has to bother the deformed-footed bird.

There is an endless number of options for when Ricardo has the time and space to make a decision. Now, I bet you expect me to go into a big, long explanation about why one choice is better than the other, but surprise! I'm not going to do that! In fact, in most cases, it's not going to matter *what* choice Ricardo actually makes. The only thing that matters is that the choice is made from a place of calm and balance within instead of from a negative self-belief.

Here's how it all breaks down:

At first, as you read through the options, it may seem like one was better than the other. But at this stage of the human-animal relationship all you're really being asked to do here is be conscious and clear in your decision making. That means your decision is all about the intention behind why it was made rather than about which particular decision was made. This will make more sense in a minute. Keep reading.

Ricardo could choose option 1 to completely avoid dealing with the challenging moment by letting things proceed as normal, activating his negative beliefs about himself. That choice is still a possibility even when a person is making a conscious decision such as this, and in some respects this could be a solid choice because this is what Ricardo knows and is comfortable with. However, this is the experience that had been producing so many "less than" feelings in Ricardo, so it may not be the best choice.

Ricardo also could choose option 2, which is to go outside in order to scare the squirrel away. The problem with this option is that it's not really much better. If Ricardo is unsuccessful in scaring the squirrel away, then he is defeated and his negative beliefs come up anyway. If he takes his eye off the ball and forgets to go outside to keep the squirrel away one time, then once again, he is unsuccessful. Since his goodness is judged based on his success here, he'll once again walk away not feeling good enough.

Ricardo also could choose option 3, to make a squirrel feeder and thereby eliminate any potential problems between the bird and the squirrel. But in the end, what option Ricardo chooses doesn't really matter.

All of Ricardo's options for handling the upcoming challenge moment could be bad choices or good choices. What the choices are actually has no bearing on Ricardo's success in this situation. The potential for success and failure lies within each. That's because it's not about what Ricardo decides to do—it's about why he decides to do it. It's about the intention behind the decision.

Remember, because Ricardo is in a state of curiosity and is able to notice that a challenge moment is about to occur, he is now sitting in his newly created moment. He still could choose to scare the squirrel away, for example, but if he does it because he needs to prove to himself that he is a good rescuer to the bird, then he didn't take advantage of the time and space created by his prediction. If, on the other hand, he stays calm and clear and remembers how much he loves watching this bird eat and wants to be outside with the bird, he's then shifting his intention behind his choices, which will lead to a new outcome. He's still keeping the squirrel away, but the reasoning behind that action has changed.

Additionally, while still in this calm and clear emotional space, Ricardo could decide that squirrels need to eat too. He would find enjoyment in making a squirrel feeder, and that's okay too. It may be the same action, but notice there is no need or proof within it; it's purely for the experience or enjoyment.

Notice that in all these options, the decisions made are no different from the above decisions, except for one major component:

there is no emotional charge. The negative belief (in Ricardo's case, of not being good enough) is not playing a role in his decision-making process anymore because he took advantage of the time and space created by his prediction. Ricardo is successfully determining his course of action *before* he's emotionally wrought, which allows him to decide how to handle things in a more factual way.

It should now be clear that the action Ricardo chooses is of much less importance than the reasoning behind why he is taking it. It's all about clear intention coming from a place of calm and peace within (as opposed to coming from an emotionally charged place), and this is what your animal is going to demand of you in this work. Even here, your animal is expecting you to do whatever it takes—to stay in curiosity mode as much as possible—to manage your emotions so that you can make the best choices for yourself. What amazing beings these animals really are!

Let Your Experiences Inform Your Beliefs

The more often you go through this new kind of decision-making process with your animal, the more often you'll have positive experiences that reinforce positive thoughts about yourself and subsequently begin chipping away at your negative beliefs. When Ricardo chooses to go outside to watch the bird purely because he loves the beautiful way she eats (rather than to prove he is a good rescuer), he is empowering himself to do something through his passion rather than through his inner need. The more Ricardo plays in his passion, the more positive experiences he's going to have, and the more those positive experiences will begin to erode his negative beliefs. So as Ricardo is enjoying himself watching the bird, he's thinking things to himself like "Oh, this is fun! And I love this" and "What a beautiful bird!" and "Oh, wow! This feels so peaceful!" Perhaps he finally notices it doesn't even look like the bird is in pain from his deformed foot. All these thoughts counteract his belief that he's not good enough.

It takes surprisingly little time to have the weight of your experiences start pointing in a new direction, thereby transforming your negative beliefs. That's the beauty of this work with your animal—each and every experience you have with her in which you make your choices consciously from that place of clarity (before the challenging moment hits) has an effect on those beliefs. It doesn't matter if that experience with your animal is a huge moment or a teeny-tiny, almost imperceptible moment—each and every experience effectively chips away at that old negative belief.

The belief change that starts happening is not an absolute, all-at-once change. It's more of a bit-by-bit shift because it's based on the various new experiences you're creating with your animal. It's easier to understand if you imagine that the negative belief shifts in small percentages. Perhaps when you first encounter your animal, 97 percent of you believes that you aren't worthy of love, but as you keep doing your work and have more and more experiences with your animal that show you you're worthy of love, that percentage goes down to 92 percent and then 87 percent and so on. Even the smallest change in what you believe about yourself changes how you think about yourself. Without you having to force it, it forever alters the choices you'll make in a very positive way. So a 5 percent change is really a very big and wonderful change!

Just like how using willpower to shift your behavior with your animal isn't an effective method for true, deep change, the differences in beliefs that arise from doing this work with your animal are not something you can *make* happen either, although your first instinct may be to do just that. (And you may be wondering, then why am I reading this book at all?) As I've said before and I'll say again, you can't talk yourself into believing that you're an awesome, loveable person if you don't believe it (even though your animal believes it!). Your beliefs about yourself were formed through your experiences. It was your experiences (interactions with other people, animals, things; words people said to you; successes and failures) that shaped the foundation for any negative beliefs you hold about yourself, so it is through your new experiences that you will have to change your beliefs.

You cannot learn the lesson your animal is helping you learn by forcing yourself to behave the way you think you should be behaving. You're not going to make yourself suddenly like yourself by telling yourself you should. Has that worked in the past? Kind of, right? As long as you kept reminding yourself that you're good or awesome or lovable or safe, you could tap a little bit into that feeling, but the moment you took your eye off that ball, the old beliefs came rushing back. So since the work with your animal is all about learning something at the deepest levels, talking yourself into it, forcing yourself to behave differently, and relying on good ol' fashioned willpower are not options here.

What will work here is continuing to experience your relationship with your animal through your newfound awareness. Put the willpower away!

I always like to say to my clients, "You can't bake a new cake with the same old ingredients!" You can't command a cake baked with your regular vanilla ingredients to become a chocolate cake just because you understand that a different flavored cake is possible. You have to slow down, keep the curiosity going, and let the moments of clarity and decision happen so that you can use some new ingredients in your cake. The more curiosity you hold with your animal, the more conscious you are in making your decisions regarding her, the more opportunity you're giving to yourself to have new, positive experiences that rewrite the old negative beliefs. This is truly why this animal is part of your life—to assist you in doing that rewriting. No one wants to walk through the world believing negative things about themselves, but the amazing creatures we allow into our lives have the ability to see into us, to understand what we think about ourselves, and to help us let go of those negative filters through the behaviors and what they inspire in us.

Animals in Action: Danielle and Kelso

Before my son was born, my husband and I decided to rescue a dog. We'd just finished up our graduate school degrees and purchased our first home. It just felt like the right time to rescue, and with us finally having a backyard of our own, we knew things were lining up well for this to happen. Kevin and I adore big dogs and always love an underdog, so we were both very attracted to pit bulls, boxers, and any other kind of dog that most people would be scared of. Over the years, I've learned that these wonderful breeds—mixed or not—have huge and loyal hearts, and Kevin loves a good lap sitting with a seventy-pound dog. Yeah, we're weird like that.

We brought ten-pound, twelve-week-old Kelso into our lives, and right away we bonded with him. He snuggled the entire trip back to our house, tucked inside my sweatshirt with only his two amber eyes and dark black nose poking out. When we arrived back at the house ninety minutes later, however, it was a different story. Up and down the stairs and then up and down again, never actually using his back legs. We guessed he felt that was just too much work!

As Kelso grew up, he became the most loyal, caring, cool dog. Always watching, always wondering, always aware of what I, Kevin, or (eventually) Cole was doing at any given moment. Kelso was seventy-three pounds of pure love and muscle. His mother had been a boxer, and we suspected his father was at least part pit bull. Whatever breeds came together to produce Kelso didn't really matter—he was just gorgeous. With his broad chest, powerful legs, and super cute mashed-up nose, we couldn't walk him down the street in our town without at least five or six different people stopping us to compliment his beauty and talk about him.

The thing about Kelso was that not only was he beautiful and powerful, he was also sensitive. Even as a puppy, he didn't like loud noises, he hated aggressive machinery (like the lawn mower), and he ran away from loud music. The other things Kelso didn't like? Anger. Negativity. Conflict. From two people angrily fighting on TV to someone cheering excitedly at a soccer game, Kelso would become visibly upset and either start shaking or try to tiptoe away from the negativity as quietly as possible. And yes, I mean tiptoe. Imagine a midnight black boxer tiptoeing down the stairs and now you have an accurate picture of Kelso.

So what do you do when you have an ultra sensitive dog? If you're paying attention, you adjust. We had to learn that we couldn't just push through Kelso's upset. We had to stop and change what we were doing. This was hard for me, as I had spent my whole life prior to this trying to push through and ignore my own sensitivity. This mind frame resulted in a major depression in high school, depression and panic attacks throughout my modeling career, and escalating panic attacks through graduate school.

Through Kelso's reactions, I learned to be more mindful of my schedule, as we found that he was happier when he knew exactly when he was going to eat, when bedtime was, when his walk was. It was like this routine helped him relax into his day. The funny thing is having a routine also helped me relax into my day. Kevin and I also had to change how we behaved in our house. Prior to Kelso, we played loud music all the time, we had friends over who liked to drink and get loud and obnoxious, and we watched crappy TV shows in which people were often angry with each other or the tension was just too high.

One show in particular, *24* with Kiefer Sutherland, made me quite anxious. The series, which focused on finding and killing the terrorists who were threatening the United States, was filmed as if it were real time, and there was always a countdown clock on the screen. I noticed that while we were watching, Kelso would become upset, shaking and cowering on his bed. It was Kevin who finally called me out for doing the exact same thing. I was constantly walking out of the room to get away from the stress of the show (this was before the days of TiVo and DVR, so I couldn't just pause). As soon as we eliminated *24* from our TV habits, I felt more relaxed and calm each evening, and clearly so did Kelso.

Kelso's sensitivity really did force me to pay attention to my own sensitivity. For years I had been trying to escape it, only to have this one seventy-pound dog enter my life and push me to deal with it. I didn't have plans to look deep within myself to discover why I was having these panic attacks. I thought, "This is just who I am." But with Kelso's assistance (he freaked out when I freaked out), I realized the panic attacks weren't who I was; they were, in fact, taking away from who I was. I wanted nothing more than for Kelso to feel light and easy in his home, so I dedicated three months to weekly acupuncture and finally rid myself of those panic attacks. Kelso definitely benefitted from this, as did Kevin and I.

Throughout his life, Kelso and his sensitivity continued to push both Kevin and me to eat more cleanly, take care of ourselves better, and really acknowledge the special people that we are. As the years wore on, I started having my students work with Kelso as well. His conscientious, unconditional love was contagious, and to this day, I still meet students who talk to me about their time with Kelso and how he helped them acknowledge and embrace their own sensitive selves.

Chapter Seven

STEP 5: MASTERY

What does it really mean to master the relationship between you and your animal? What does it really mean to transform negative beliefs by working with your animal? Does it mean that you'll never have any challenges with your animal again? Does it mean that your animal now behaves perfectly all the time? Does it mean that this animal will only inspire you, rather than cause negative emotions, from this point forward? Does it mean that you're now "fixed" and will have no more problems in your life? The answer to every single one of those questions is simply no.

When you master the relationship you have with this very special animal, many different things can happen. The challenges or hot buttons between the two of you often smooth out, but they will never be erased completely. Animals of all types—wild, pet, zoo, teaching, and other—are working every day to keep us on our toes, whether we're in the midst of learning the lesson or we're on the tail end of really getting it.

When we slip our behavior, thoughts, emotions, and actions back toward that which isn't serving us, you can bet that animal is going to show up one way or another to get you back in line. If hearing about a particular animal killed through canned hunting moved you to start donating time and energy to animal activism and to align yourself with people, experiences, groups, events, and causes that assist you in that direction, then you can bet that when you start associating with someone who is out of that alignment, that original particular animal will show up for you again to remind you of your purpose and newfound enlightenment. Perhaps you'll be scrolling through Facebook and a story will show up in your newsfeed that focuses on some new aspect of that killing, or perhaps a friend at dinner will mention canned hunting to you. However it happens, the animals are going to keep you in line and on track—if you keep watching out for the signs.

It doesn't matter how far along you are on the journey or how much you've mastered, the animals, all of them, are aware, watching, and working every moment of every day. In many ways, mastery of the relationship with your animal doesn't really allow for a letting go or a stopping or a "phew!" It more allows for a time when you can relax a little bit into what you've learned and what you're creating. Just know that if you fall off track with your newfound awareness, that animal is going to let you know!

So far, this book has shown you many things. First, it's helped you explore a deeper relationship with an animal that profoundly affects your life. Second, you've come to see how this animal is constantly helping you evolve in a particular area and how the animal assistance can change your life when you're inspired to accept it and run with it. And third, this book has shown you how what you're learning about yourself through your animal will benefit you not only in the relationship with your animal but also in other areas of your life as well.

As you begin to master the ins and outs of the relationship with your animal, though, the changes that occur can be very subtle. So subtle, in fact, that you might even ask yourself, "Did any changes really occur?" In fact, often nothing monumental has actually occurred in your life. Not with you and not with this special animal being who has been assisting you along the way. Or at least it will seem that way at first glance. If you find yourself in this position now (this is a very common experience), it's a very good thing.

As you master the lesson your animal is teaching you—when your negative filters about yourself are dissolving away and being replaced with positive beliefs about yourself—there is no way that your life will not change. It will. It absolutely will.

But utterly without fanfare.

Through curiosity and conscious decision-making, you've simply but definitively begun changing the negative beliefs driving your thoughts and behaviors, and in their place grow happy, healthy, creative, supportive beliefs. You may have struggled to trust you could be good at anything before Bobo came into your life and forced you to address that conviction, but now, at this stage, believing in yourself is starting to seem almost ... normal. Of course you're going to try out that obstacle course race with your dog. Maybe you'll finish, maybe you won't, but it will be a fun and great experience for both of you. Whether or not that experience has any bearing on your inherent goodness or worthiness isn't really on the table as a question anymore. It's just a dog obstacle course. Do you or don't you want to run it?

When your beliefs change, your decision-making process changes as well. If you inherently believe that you're a pretty awesome person, there is a whole lot less "deciding" that has to happen. Either the obstacle course race sounds enjoyable or it doesn't. Neither of these answers has anything to do with your goodness, worthiness, or lovability, and at this point, it would begin to seem really weird if they did.

That drama—"Am I good enough to do it?" or "I'll never win" or "I don't want other people to see me struggle"—or whatever old commotion prevented you from choosing to take on that obstacle course with your dog is finally (or mostly) gone because your experiences have devalued it. And while that sounds like a wonderful and even inspiring idea (No drama? Count me in!), it can be very scary for many people. It means there are no more obstacles standing in the way. It means that you do have to take your dog for a walk every day because you have mastered leash work after you've started believing in yourself. But do you really want to have to go on a dog walk every day? What about the weather? What about when you're tired? It was almost easier when you couldn't take her because she was so unruly. In other words, the results of shifting how you think, feel, react, and believe through this work with your animal are so all-encompassing that many people get almost all the way through to the mastery phase and then try to quit.

When change happens, it happens. Change that takes place at the core of your being is not something you have to keep an eye on; it is just there. Many people experiencing resistance will question whether the changes that are happening are worth allowing so much of their life—and often their personality—to shift. They start worrying about losing who they really are and actually begin to battle the transformations that are already occurring within as their beliefs are changing, perhaps even abandoning their curiosity/awareness process.

I'm probably dating myself here, but in the 1987 movie *The Witches of Eastwick* (I love my '80s movies) Jack Nicholson, who plays the role of the devil, is finally almost defeated. Through magic spells, he's reduced to a small creature-like thing that is melting away. But even as he's melting away, he's fighting to stay alive. This is very much like the resistance that so many people at this stage will feel. It's the old beliefs doing anything they can to remain in power: Your dog won't love you if you have rules! You can't make enough money to send your horse to that awesome stable! You're never going to find anyone who will love you other than your rabbit!

Fortunately for us, and unfortunately for those beliefs, our positive beliefs are much stronger. Your curiosity and newfound understanding of yourself will overcome any resistance those old beliefs are throwing in your way. The animal in your life will ensure that, as you grow, your personal positive outlook grows, and in exchange, the relationship with your special animal will grow as well. While your cat used to hiss at visitors all the time, she'll begin greeting them with a quiet meow from across the room. While your favorite goat used to shy away from you whenever you approached the barn, he'll now show signs of warming. The further you move into this mastery place, where you believe yourself to be the positive, protected, wonderful, deserving, loving being you are, the more incredible the changes and growth will continue to occur between you and this special animal.

There is something very cool yet at the same time completely unnoticeable that happens between you and your animal once you've been working on this process for a little bit. I call it mastery, but that wording may be a little strong. When it happens it is a huge deal, but also you tend to overlook it. I know it may seem like I'm contradicting myself, but I'm really not!

Let's say that your animal, Larry the wild bobcat, has been working with you to help you believe in yourself more. With each little bit of belief in your own power, Larry comes onto your property and kills fewer chickens. Well, since this process is going on over a few weeks, by the end of that time, you probably won't even notice that Larry has stopped killing your chickens because it seems so normal to *not* have him killing your chickens and to feel this sense of power within you.

When you reach this mastery phase, things are the way they are. It will seem so typical that you may forget that things were ever any different with your animal. For me, my mastery with another one of my dogs, Bella, showed up in the form of forgetting to consider the "Bella jumping problem" before inviting friends over. As she helped me change my belief in myself and as I started to feel that I really am a pretty great person, it became just an ordinary part of our lives that we would have people we wanted to hang out with over to our house. I didn't spend time preparing Bella for friends to come over and didn't worry that I wouldn't be able to control her. Bella, in fact, wasn't part of my thought process at all on that subject, and that was exactly the way it should be. Because my belief about myself had changed deeply and thoroughly, I didn't have to focus on it anymore. I didn't have to worry about myself and my power or Bella and her behavior: all of that had changed because my belief had changed, and so I was placing myself in the world from my inner power rather than my inner fears.

But this can all be very anticlimactic. I know

I pretty quickly forgot that Bella used to jump up on everyone and go nuts when people came over because she wasn't doing it anymore. A dog is supposed to calmly greet people, wag her tail, and say hi—and that's what she was doing, so I didn't give it two thoughts. But when I finally *did* pause for a moment to re-member how it used to be, I was able to see that things in my life had drastically changed. When your belief changes to the positive version, it just makes so much more sense! And it's easier too. You don't think, "I'm so glad I'm about to trust myself," you just trust yourself. It's natural. It's just the way it goes.

So here you are: you've been working with your animal; you've been allowing her to show you into your soul, using her messages to help you manage your energy; and you've been looking to her to help you become truly curious about yourself and your crazy decisions. With all that work with your animal, there is no way that change hasn't happened. The problem is that many of you aren't going to think about it—you're just going to go on with your ev-eryday (changed) life, feeling that it's normal and forgetting to look back and see what you did.

It's important to celebrate that you have shifted through this relationship with your animal! Try to remember how it used to be with your animal. Think back to those emotions you held or the feelings you avoided or the thoughts you didn't like that you had. When I'm working with a private client, this is usually the point when I advise doing something to celebrate the changes that have come. When things are good, we so often forget to look back and feel grateful for how far we've come. I fall into this pattern as well, being caught up in the now and in what's ahead versus giving my-self a moment to notice all that I've accomplished. This is not ego overpowering you; this is you taking the time to give yourself and your animal the credit you both deserve for shifting yourself into the positive.

And it is through this positive place that you'll not only feel happier, more content, less anxious, and more love for yourself, but you'll also be open now to experiencing a higher level of consciousness, empathy, understanding, and love for everyone else as well, either human or animal, because you'll be feeling this from within. And what we feel from within radiates outward into our experience, our environment, and our worlds.

True Change

True change that stays with you throughout the rest of your life— no matter what your circumstances, no matter who is around you, no matter what other people say—occurs because your beliefs about yourself have actually changed. Your animal taps into this, understands this, and works with you to inspire, shock, and excite you into creating new beliefs through your experiences. We've been talking a lot about these four core erroneous beliefs that people hold about themselves: I'm not safe/supported/protected, I'm not good enough, I'm not deserving/worthy, and I'm not loveable. When the change you make within actually transforms these from negative to positive, everything in your life will shift, beginning with the relationship with your animal and continuing outward into every single other area of your life. This is the type of change you're working toward with your animal and the type of change that arises out of this new way of being with yourself.

As you've probably realized, working with your animal is an ongoing process, one that will continue as long as this animal is part of your life and, for many, even after the animal has left your life. The skills you've learned through working in this manner with your animal don't just apply to your animal anymore. Most people start applying them to their human-human relationships, to their career, to their family, and more. And I believe that that's what animals want us to do—they certainly want us to evolve ourselves into magnificent souls that are able to access our greatness every day. But they don't want us to stop there. They want us to take this greatness we've discovered and spread it out to the rest of the world by holding compassion for others who haven't yet discovered it, feeling grateful for the animals that are working so hard to help us learn about our greatness, and just plain living that greatness every day.

While this book has been all about you and your animal, as you expand into seeing who you really are, it will affect your entire being. In turn, that will affect everyone who comes into contact with you. In this way, the animals of the world are working, very effectively, to shift human consciousness, making us into the people we really are—wonderful, compassionate, and unconditionally loving of ourselves and of others.

Animal-Assisted Therapy

The easiest way to understand and accept animals as our teachers is to see the phenomenon in action. Let's take a look at something you're probably more familiar with: therapy animals. Through animal-assisted therapy, which often takes place in hospitals and rehabilitation centers, the goal is to improve a patient's social, emotional, or cognitive functioning using animals as the "treatment." Animals employed in this type of therapy may be dogs, cats, horses, guinea pigs—pretty much any kind of animal that a person can feel affection for or bond with. The therapy that occurs between the person and the animal ranges from the animal simply hanging around with a recovering patient, to the patient caring for the animal in some way or performing a particular task with the animal. There are so many ways that animals help humans that how the therapy is carried out is very much based on the skills of the animal and the specific needs of the human.

There are programs all over the United States and even throughout the world that aim to take advantage of the innate soft spot most people hold in their hearts for animals. I've seen therapy dogs brought into nursing homes to cuddle and bond with the residents, which creates excitement and something to look forward to for the residents and a profound sense of love between the person and animal. I read about two dogs, both born without their front legs, who were adopted by a family and trained to become therapy dogs. Now, their owners take them on trips to hospitals and hospice centers where they buzz around in their specialized dog wheelchairs, greeting patients and lifting the hearts of all those they come in contact with.

Yes, this really is a form of therapy! In fact, working with animals is so universally transformational that many other programs that focus on inmates and dogs have since sprung up in prisons around the country. The training of the dogs by the inmates is usually a great success, but the even bigger success is the emotional transformation in the inmates chosen to train the dogs: they became happier, healthier, and more positive, and they typically leave prison with a newfound purpose.

In California, there is another program taking advantage of the healing that happens between a person and an animal. Rescued wolves are paired with veterans coping with PTSD—in fact, the rescued wolf *chooses* which veteran he or she will be bonded with, and the two will spend hours together in the woods, just being together and caring for one another. The participants have said that their time with their wolf partner taught them the skills they needed to reenter the world: how to be calm, assertive, and more confident. This is an amazing feat when you consider that the veterans are just "hanging out" with and caring for their wolf.

Working deeply and emotionally with animals is already a well-documented form of healing that has had a lot of mainstream success. This book takes animal therapy to a new level that is much deeper, more profound, and more easily attainable for the everyday person. When working with your animal as your teacher, you don't have to be ill, suffering from PTSD, or in prison in order to work with an animal to access your best you. You only have to want to achieve something in your life (more happiness, a better job, a more passionate relationship, less worry) and have an animal to whom you feel connected. Animal Lessons makes healing, growing, and expanding through your animal accessible to a much wider audience—you!

Animal Lessons takes advantage of your love of animals to help you achieve your best life. By taking stock of your relationship with the animal you love—what upsets you about her, what puzzles you about her, how she makes you feel, what you experience through her—and by learning to work with that information through her, you'll be able to make changes in yourself and in your life more easily and with much less effort. And crazily enough, I'm not overstating what this system can do for you.

Animals in Action

The following stories are a few examples from people who have worked with animals in this way to change the course of their life.

Rhea and Dolly

Rhea was a computer programmer who typically worked eighty to ninety hours per week. She would come home exhausted each night and crash into bed until the next morning, when she would wake up and do it all over again. For months her cat, Dolly, had been suffering from hairballs due to overgrooming, and Rhea had been forced to make frequent trips to the vet to get help for Dolly.

When I first met Rhea, she was at her wit's end with Dolly and vet visits. She couldn't figure out how to control the situation and how to help Dolly get better and stay better. The suggestions and medications from her vet to curb the overgrooming were not working, and Dolly was clearly unhappy and uncomfortable. When Rhea brought Dolly to me, I intuited what was going on and explained this to her. Dolly's overgrooming was directed at Rhea, who wasn't taking care of herself and was instead dedicating all her time to her work. Rhea was surprised that her cat would care whether or not she took care of herself, but felt she was out of other "more logical" options and decided to make a change in her life. She told me she had nothing to lose by listening to her cat's message (since everything else she had tried had failed) and began following the first step in the program.

As Rhea went through each of the Animal Lessons steps with Dolly, she noticed that the better she took care of herself (working fewer hours, getting massages, going to the movies), the less troublesome Dolly's hairball situation became. Interestingly (and not surprisingly), Rhea's other life challenges also began to even out as the work with Dolly forced her to create balance in her life. Within a few months, Rhea had made two new friends, and she found herself enjoying leaving work to meet her new friends for dinner. Paralleling that change for the better, Dolly's hairball problem had alleviated as well.

Mike and Fly

Mike consulted me because his dog Fly was excessively shy. He was concerned because Fly didn't interact with any of the other dogs in his home and didn't want to hang out with people other than Mike. When I first met Fly, it seemed that Mike was right. It took quite some time with Fly for me to gain his trust, but once Fly opened to me, I saw that he viewed his life with Mike very differently from how Mike viewed his life with Fly.

Fly wasn't super shy. Fly wasn't shy at all. In fact, the challenge, according to what Fly showed me, was that Mike had an anxiety problem and Fly could feel this and didn't want to be around all the worry. Mike's anxiety was twice as bad whenever friends visited the house or when the other dogs approached Fly.

It surprised Mike to learn that it was his own anxiety that was causing the problem. Until that time, he'd always seen his anxiety as just part of who he was, somewhat like a personality trait. He accepted that he stayed up late at night thinking about every possible angle on a situation and that he needed to be early wherever he went because being late made him worry. It had never occurred to Mike that his worry would be something that Fly would notice or even be affected by. Mike decided to give my Animal Lessons process a try. He didn't want Fly to be uncomfortable because of his own anxiety by realizing he didn't feel safe, supported, and protected in the world.

As Mike moved through the steps with Fly and discovered and found success alleviating and preventing his own anxiety, Fly, in turn, began to behave more comfortably in social situations. With Fly as his anxiety barometer, Mike now meditates every day for fifteen minutes, and he's begun karate lessons to "get out" any lingering worry. Mike's happier disposition and newfound belief that he is safe in the world has also helped him become more social, giving Fly, who has come out of his shell in tandem, plenty of opportunities to play with others (both animal and human).

Tom and Whiskers

When Tom was nine years old, he convinced his mom to buy him a rabbit from the 4-H club at the farmer's market in his hometown. The rabbit had soft, beautiful, white fur that he loved to mush his fingers through, and he promptly became Tom's very best friend. Tom named him Whiskers but called him Wisk for short. Tom would take Wisk on walks in the backyard on his leash, let him loose in the house so that he could get exercise, and let him play throughout the day with the family guinea pig, Sunshine, for fun. The duo really seemed to like each other and would scamper through the house together, hiding under furniture and chewing on random wires.

A few months after Wisk came into Tom's life, his parents called his brother and him into the living room where they swiftly and seemingly spontaneously (to Tom's nine-year-old ears) announced that they were getting a divorce. To Tom, this was the worst thing that ever could have happened, and he ran to his bedroom—straight to Wisk—feeling devastated and alone. Tom's dad was moving out of the house, and Tom felt abandoned.

All kids handle divorce differently. Some kids act out and start causing trouble, while others might start doing poorly in school. Tom's brother, who was three years younger than him, became sullen and angry and very needy with his mother for the next few years. It was clear that he felt abandoned by the situation as well and wanted to receive enough love from their mom to make up for the loss of love from their absent dad. Tom chose a different route.

Nine years old is fourth grade. And Tom has very particular memories from that year: a girl in his class stood up and read a story she wrote about the word hate. She didn't like the word hate and she refused to use it, because she didn't really think it was possible to hate. For some reason, that had always stuck with him, probably because fourth grade was the first time he'd ever really experienced hate. Fourth grade is also when Tom decided to stop talking. To humans, that is. Sure, he answered when adults spoke directly to him, and when his therapist wanted him to talk, he talked. But, for most of his day, he kept his head down and tried to go through unnoticed, as if he could become invisible and escape his feelings of abandonment and of not feeling good enough to keep his dad around.

It's hard for any young kid to go without anyone to talk to, and as a result, Wisk became his confidant. After school, he would walk through the door of his house, throw his backpack down next to the stairs and immediately make his way down the hallway to the rabbit cage in the backyard so that they could spend time together. If they had good weather, Tom would take him outside and sit in the grass or talk to him about how he was the only one in his life who really understood. It was Wisk's never-ending interest and devotion to Tom that helped Tom see that, regardless of his father leaving his life, he was still loveable—even if it was just this little white creature twitching his nose and running across his lap to grab a carrot.

As Wisk grew a year older, Tom began to feel more comfortable with himself. Wisk's continued interest in Tom boosted the self-confidence that had been shot by his father's leaving. By fifth grade, a classmate named Janine was telling Tom how popular he was in fourth grade because he was so mysterious by not talking. Ah, how kids translate things!

But for Tom, his relationship with Wisk had opened something up within him that had not really been there before. Wisk taught him that although some people in life were going to disappoint him, there were others who were dependable, sticking with him through the good times and the bad. Wisk stuck by him, showing him that he really was worthy of love. His repeated experience with Wisk of receiving love and support counteracted the experience of abandonment from his father. When I spoke with Tom about this, he said that to this day, he feels that the love of his rabbit is what kept him from going down the road of not believing he was worthy of love. He still, as a forty-five-year-old man, expresses great gratitude toward Wisk for his unending love and devotion.

Candy and Leila

My client Candy was concerned about her cat Leila because Leila was tossing the other cats in the house, counter surfing, destroying the garbage in the kitchen, and generally being a bully. Candy was particularly upset by Leila's behavior because prior to that year, Leila had been the sweetest, most easygoing cat of all the cats in the house. Candy wanted nothing more than to bring back the sweetie pie cat Leila had been for the eight years before.

After checking with her vet to ensure that Leila did not have a medical problem that had caused the change in her behavior, Candy began working with Animal Lessons to try and shift the situation in the household. Within a week of beginning this work, Candy finally began to appreciate that Leila was being overly vocal about what she wanted because Candy herself was not being vocal at all. Candy had been in a relationship for several years in which she was not speaking up about her real needs and wants with her partner. She also had a situation going on at work in which she was allowing her business partner to take advantage of her rather than acknowledging that she didn't think the behavior was appropriate. Leila was modeling *extreme* speaking up until Candy could shift her beliefs and start doing it for herself.

Candy knew she had to change this pattern within if she ever wanted Leila to start getting along with the other cats—and if she ever wanted to feel supported in her relationship and at work. Determined to shift things with Leila, Candy started seeing a therapist, reading self-help books, and working with a life coach, in addition to working directly with Leila. Her goal was to master the art of standing up for herself. Excitingly, as Candy started to believe she was more valuable in the world and improved at speaking up, Leila's bullying behavior subsequently subsided. Today, Leila and Candy have a newfound understanding for each other, and Candy is standing up for what she believes in with more ease and grace than she ever thought possible.

Opportunities for Growth

In all three stories, the people involved were able to recognize that a challenge they were having with their pet was actually an opportunity for their own growth, which would in turn better the life of their pet as well. If they had not been open to this idea, however, they would most likely have had a much more difficult time in their respective situations. Rhea may have spent thousands more dollars at the veterinarian trying to figure out how to get Dolly to stop over grooming, when all she really had to do was start taking care of herself. Mike might have become a recluse, using the excuse that Fly couldn't handle social situations (while really hiding his own anxiety), and Candy may have had to rehome bully Leila instead of learning the art of standing up for herself.

I've seen people work with the Animal Lessons steps to finally leave a bad relationship, overcome anxiety, stop believing they are worthless, let go of having to be number one, finally feel comfortable showing themselves to the world, stop losing themselves in their loved ones, earn promotions, get better jobs, come out to their friends and family, and become truly happy for the first time in their lives. The list of things that you can achieve by working with your animal is unlimited.

Chapter Eight

ENERGY MANAGEMENT

I've included this chapter because it's like the secret ingredient to success. If you can employ the tools and techniques I show you in this chapter throughout your work with your animal, it's going to make everything easier, smoother, clearer—and yes, faster! Energy management is one of my favorite things to teach because I've both experienced personally and witnessed in thousands of clients the powerful shifts that it can make. You, on the other hand, will probably want to ignore this chapter feeling that you don't need it, but I want to strongly impress upon you how valuable energy management is to the entire Animal Lessons process! Most people immediately discount the idea of managing their energy either as something that is unnecessary or as something only hippies from the '60s would ever do. They believe they can power through their emotions without bothering to deal with them. I, on the other hand, look at energy management as the biggest key to success in working with animals and really in any internal, consciousness self-work. Yes, it's *that* important!

In almost any class I'm teaching—whether it's about animal communication, animals and the other side, guru animals, soul contracts, relationship improvement, or anything else—there is always at least a pretty firm nod toward energy management. Energy management, for the purposes of this book (and for the purposes of all work that I do), is simply working to maintain an emotional, mental, and energetic balance within yourself. When you are in a place of the best balance (what I like to call "the zone"), you'll find that you can make decisions more easily; you'll have deeper, more complete relationships; you'll feel better and believe better about yourself; and overall, you'll experience your life as easier. And this is no exaggeration of what energy management can do for you.

Balance is the most crucial aspect of energy management, but it probably doesn't look like you would expect. Think of someone walking on a balance beam. They spread their arms out to the side and wobble a little bit, to the left and right, to maintain their balance as they go. This is exactly how energy management works. It is not a consistent feeling of total calm and awesomeness within that never changes. Instead, it is constant adjustments, some large and some small, all coming together to create the balance. A little happier, a little less upset, a little more determined … each of these things is an emotional adjustment that you'll make as you strive to find your balance again and again and again.

When you lack energetic and emotional balance, it can be very difficult to do your work with your animal, and it can also be a challenge just to make it through your day. When you allow yourself to be overcome by money anxiety, to worry that so-and-so doesn't like you, or to feel chaos throughout your home, you're missing the opportunity to balance your energy and benefit from the lessons behind these things instead. Additionally, when your energy isn't balanced—when you feel a sense of dread about your job, for example—you may find it difficult to see things clearly and make good decisions.

Imagine you are hanging out with your best friend Sherry, and you're both in pharmaceutical drug sales. Now, Sherry, being the "talker" that she is, talks at you for twenty minutes about her incredible sales record. She mentions that the head of the company sought her out the other day to personally congratulate her and how several other companies are courting her. As you are listening to this, let's say it strikes a nerve and you begin to feel inadequate. You're listening to her and nodding your head, but inside you're thinking, "Why doesn't anyone congratulate me? I wish that would happen for me!" and other similar thoughts. That downward spiral of thought and the negative emotions that come along with it aren't signs that you are a horrible salesperson who is inappropriately jealous of your friend's success. Instead these thoughts are signs, specific messages from your body, that it's time to manage your energy and bring yourself back into balance.

When you're sitting in negative emotions like jealousy and victimhood as described in the example with Sherry above, it becomes very hard to make a decision that is truly for your greatest and highest good about how to react, what to say, and even around what you feel. Here you are, stewing in this jealousy, knowing that the "right" thing to do is to support your friend Sherry and her success at her job—do you really think you're going to handle this situation in the best possible way? The answer is no. Of course you're not going to make great decisions about this! If you feel this jealousy, ignore it, and say, "That's great, Sherry," now you're not only ignoring your own feelings, you're also being untrue to what you're experiencing within. If you decide to say nothing instead, you'll be censoring yourself and your feelings and potentially making Sherry feel bad about her own success.

When you manage your energy because you're experiencing something that is upsetting you, the energy management itself will soften or shift this upset and replace it with thoughts, feelings, and emotions that are more helpful to your situation. In the Sherry example, instead of continuing to feel jealous, you could come to a place of acceptance around her success and feel genuine happiness for her while also using that acceptance and happiness to motivate you to push yourself a bit more in the future, or perhaps you could say to her, "Wow, I'm so impressed! I'm jealous, but I'm also impressed!"

But this takes real, solid energy management. Not "name only" energy management. How many times have you read in a book about a great grounding exercise, heard a friend talk about a new meditation that she just loves, or listened to someone on Oprah's *SuperSoul Sunday* mention their new technique accessing the stillness within—and then you've followed their directions to a tee, but that calm never occurred within you? This phenomenon is something that I see all the time in my private practice. You could learn about the hottest energy management tool from the coolest, biggest name in the self-help industry, you could set out to practice it and become obsessed with doing it well, you could make a complete and utter commitment to it, and yet it could just plain not work for you.

Every energy management technique does not work for every person, just like every type of physical exercise does not work to get every person in shape. It's that simple. As you're learning about energy management, you want to pay strong attention to whether or not the technique *actually* worked. Did you really feel calmer afterward? Did it really help you come into a place of more clarity within, or do you feel better mostly because you followed directions and did what is *supposed* to make you feel more grounded? Doing something because you're supposed to, because it's what you committed to, because everyone else is gaining positive experiences from it, or because of any reason other than it actually had the desired positive effect is not true energy management. That's following the rules for the sake of the rules rather than developing the awareness of yourself within to determine if what you're doing is having the desired effect. What really counts in energy management is that whatever weird, crazy thing you chose to do is something that can create an emotional, energetic, and mental change for the better within you.

Interestingly though, true energy management means you can never operate on autopilot. Once you find something that works for you, something that restores you to a place of balance within, or something that makes you feel peaceful and happy, that tool may not continue to work for you indefinitely or even consistently. In fact, it's very likely that that tool will only work some of the time! Energy management tools are based on your own energetic and emotional state, and this isn't something that can be fudged. If you're at an 8 for anxiety on a scale of 1–10, with 10 being an insane amount of anxiety, you're going to choose a very different tool for rebalancing than if you're at a 4. The tool that balances you at an 8 will most likely be a big-gun tool, and it may even take a little longer to complete than the tool that balances you at a 4, which might just be a quickie that you can do while sitting in your cubicle at the office.

Energy management is certainly about the tools you choose to use, but there is another component to it. This component creates the success and will pay off for you as you work with your animal and develop it: awareness. How can you decide what tool to use to manage your energy if you don't realize that your energy is in need of management? It's important that you are always paying attention to how you're feeling rather than just running through the motions of what has worked in the past.

There are so many people in the world who believe how they feel emotionally and mentally throughout the day is the only option. If they think about it at all, they think, "It is what it is, and this is just the way I am." Many anxious people, for example, believe their anxiety is simply part of their personality. Many angry people consider themselves as just that, angry. If you asked these people to describe themselves, most of them would describe that unmanaged energy as their personality. "I'm a very anxious person" or "I get mad at the drop of a hat" would feel pretty normal to these people to say. This really isn't the case, though. We are not our emotions. My emotions do not make me who I am, and I ensure, every day, that by managing my energy, my emotions do not drive my decisions or run the show. But to do this well, you have to have an awareness of what unmanaged energy is and when it is showing up. To manage your energy and to work well with your animal, you're going to have to develop an awareness of yourself that most people go their whole life without developing—not because it's hard to do, but because they have no idea it is something to be done at all.

When personal energy is functioning well, the average person will feel clear, calm, balanced, and powerful, and this is the state that we're all striving to be in as much as possible. That person who is energetically balanced will also feel happiness, confidence, and many other positive emotions. And it's when we're in this emotional/energetic state that we're really functioning at our best.

Challenges arise in every person's life, however, and these challenges often throw off a person's energy. This is very natural, but if you don't know how to handle it, those challenges and the subsequent wonky emotional/energetic state that results can start to guide your life in very negative ways. Think of a time when you've been in a good mood, feeling pretty optimistic about your life and enjoying your day, only to end up spending time with someone who is a Negative Ninny. You know the type—they view everything through a "poor me" filter, for example. After a little bit of hanging out with the Negative Ninny, you're probably feeling less positive, maybe a little more angry, and even a bit down. As a result of hanging out with this person, you may even feel off for days! This is because your wonderful, balanced energy has been disrupted by the energy of the Negative Ninny, and unless you do something about it, you could stay feeling "off" for quite some time.

Your emotions are always reflected in your energetic state, so I tend to use these two words interchangeably. For example, if your emotions are angry, your energetic state will most likely reflect that by bouncing all over the place. Similarly, if you're feeling insecure, your energy will be small and hidden, reflecting how you're feeling that lack of confidence. When you are fully in the zone, your energy looks beautiful. Imagine that you have all these sparkles around you—silver, gold, and full of light. (In my mind, they look very much like the sparks flying off a child's Fourth of July sparkler.) Those sparks are organized, and they move in unison around your body, following a kind of inner flow and dance.

When you're angry, those sparks take on that angry energy emanating from you, and they begin moving as if they are angry. Similarly, when you are sad, the sparks move as if they are depressed, traveling slowly and more erratically around your body. I know it may seem weird to think of your energy in this manner, but understanding it through this lens will help you develop a fuller, deeper awareness of yourself and your emotions so that you can go deeper in your human-animal relationship work.

There's another thing that happens as we go through our day: some of our sparks can get left off in other places. Let's say you had a particularly upsetting conversation with your boss, you got very angry with the man in the grocery store, or another car almost hit you and startled you while you were backing your car out of the parking spot. When something like this happens, we tend to scatter some of our energy. You'll know when you've done this because it usually happens through an emotional moment. Another sign that you've scattered your energy is simply that you feel chaotic or like you can't quite get a handle on things in your life.

All of this means that your energy is affecting your emotions, and your emotions are affecting your energy. Luckily for us, it also means that when you shift one of those, you'll be shifting the other. Also luckily for us, returning your energy and emotions to their best, most calm, in-the-zone state isn't very hard; it just takes knowing what to do and then actually doing it. (I have met people who have learned about this but never moved into the actual managing the energy part. Your energy will not be managed just because you learn that it needs to be. It requires you to take the real-life steps.)

I'm going to show you what it feels like when you're in your most calm, clear, balanced state possible so that you can have a baseline to compare yourself to. You'd be amazed at how many people have never experienced themselves in this amazing, peaceful, powerful energetic state and in fact had no idea that it was even possible. I'm going to teach you two very simple, very potent tools for bringing yourself back to center. The first tool will be a little more familiar than the second tool. When you move into the second technique, get ready! You'll need to suspend your belief a bit and put yourself into a "just go with the flow" mindset. This is because what I have to show you is goofy, slightly awkward, and maybe even a little embarrassing. But on the flip side, it's really helpful!

Belly Breathing Technique

This first exercise is simple, and yet not exactly. When people who are stressed out, fearful, anxious, worried, or scared breathe, they tend to use only the top part of their lungs. This is because when our bodies move into fight-or-flight mode (something has happened and you need to either take it on or run away), our breathing follows suit. Imagine running around a track. As you increase your speed, it gets harder and harder to take long, slow, deep breaths. The faster you run, the more your body naturally wants to move into shorter breathing that is higher in your chest.

While breathing high up in your chest works well in times of stress, it doesn't work so well for relaxation. Short, high breaths do not promote relaxation. Just give it a try right now to see what I mean. Put the book down, close your eyes, and start taking quick, fast, short breaths. Try to do this for a full minute and then stop and notice how you feel. Do you feel relaxed? Do you feel calm? Probably not—in fact, after breathing like this in a non-stressful situation, many people will say they feel light-headed, dizzy, more anxious, and even irritable.

The other challenge that people run into around their breathing is simply habit—and in this case, it's bad habits. The mind doesn't make a distinction between stress and anxiety caused by an environmental factor (for example, a car driving toward you erratically as you are crossing the street) and an emotional factor (such as lying in bed worrying about money). Both of these experiences can activate the fight or flight response with you, which means both of these experiences will cause your breathing pattern to change from normal (longer, slower breaths) to fight-or-flight breathing (the shorter, high, choppy breaths we've been talking about). This means that more often than you realize, you're probably doing fight-or-flight breathing—even when it's not necessarily necessary. You certainly don't need to prepare to fight when you're lying in bed worrying about the bills!

The Belly Breathing Technique will teach you how to use your breathing to move out of any fight-or-flight response in order to reach a place of calm and clarity. It's very simple, but simple doesn't always mean easy! If you're someone who has been unknowingly breathing at the top of your lungs for years, it could turn out to be just a little tricky to master the technique. But once you rid yourself of this bad habit, you'll find that it's easier than ever to bring yourself into that state of calm.

Before beginning the technique, take stock of yourself. How do you feel right now in this very moment? How does your body feel? How do your thoughts move? Would you describe them as focused? Linear? Jumpy? Chaotic? It's always a great idea to know your starting point before you do any technique because that is what will let you most successfully evaluate the effectiveness of what you've done afterward.

Once you've taken stock, you're ready to begin. The first few times you perform this technique, you probably want to be alone, free of distractions. This is solely because you're going to need to concentrate, and a TV or a boss in the background can easily pull attention from what you're doing. Start by placing the palms of each hand against the sides of your rib cage. As you look down at your torso, it might look like you've placed your hands in such a way as to squeeze your rib cage smaller, but that is not what we're going to do.

Now, with your eyes closed, begin to inhale through your nose. As you inhale through your nose, expand your ribs outward. As you do this, your hands will move outward as well. Imagine that within your ribs is a balloon that you are filling with your inhalation. Remember to keep this breath long and slow. When you have fully inhaled, just pause for a moment and then simply exhale through your mouth. As you exhale, your ribs and hands should return to the starting position.

People often run into challenges with this breathing technique because that pesky ol' fight-or-flight habit is hanging on. When your breathing is guided by the fight-or-flight response, your inhalation also pulls your stomach *in* not out, as I'm talking about here. Pulling your stomach in on the inhalation is what allows someone to breathe in the top of their lungs. You may find that my asking you to expand your ribcage on the inhalation feels exactly backward—and if that's the case for you, you simply need to retrain your breathing back to normal through the Belly Breathing Technique. Yes, that's right—the Belly Breathing Technique is really only helping you remember what normal, relaxed, healthy breathing is like.

Try belly breathing now for five to seven breaths. It may take you a few breaths to get the hang of it, but there is no hurry here. In fact, hurrying belly breathing would be the opposite of what I'm teaching you. Remember to go long and slow, inhale through your nose, and allow your ribcage to expand. Pause. Slowly exhale and allow your ribcage to return to normal. Your hands can act as a visual guide as you practice, but don't worry. Eventually, you won't need your hands, and you'll be able to use this tool wherever you are without looking crazy.

When you have spent thirty seconds or so performing the technique well, you can simply stop. Keeping your eyes closed (in the beginning—as you get better you can open your eyes), go back and take stock of how you feel. How does your body feel? How does your breathing feel? How are the thoughts moving through your head? How does the air around you feel? If you notice any changes in this, those changes are most likely going to be positive, such as feeling calmer, softer, taller, easier, stronger … and they are a sign that you are in the zone and good to go. If you don't feel any changes, you may need to redo the tool or you may need to move on to another tool, such as the Star Wars Rewind Tool, which I'm about to teach you next.

Please know that there will be days when you can do belly breathing for ten seconds, it will reset your energy, and you'll feel great. There will be other days when you can do belly breathing four times in a row, and you're just not getting into the zone. That is okay, and that is why I'm teaching you another technique. In the end, anything that you can do that helps you feel calmer, more peaceful, easier, and more thoughtful could be considered an energy management technique. What I'm teaching you here is just what I've found works best for the greatest number of people.

Star Wars Rewind Tool

If you're aware of pop culture in any way and if you're an adult of pretty much any age, you've probably heard of or seen the Star Wars movies. This tool builds on something that is very common in the Star Wars, Star Trek, and Battlestar Galactica series, as well as pretty much any other movie in which ships travel through space and shoot each other. Even if you haven't seen one of these movies, I'm sure you can imagine one ship shooting at another ship in space, and when the shot hits, the targeted ship explodes, scattering its pieces all throughout the universe. Just look up something like "Death Star explosion original" on YouTube to get a good visual of what I'm talking about here, as this is the principle we're going to use for this tool.

Except we're going to do it backward.

Before you close your eyes to begin this exercise, imagine you're a ship in space and you've been hit by an enemy missile or laser or whatever it is that you're thinking of. Upon impact, bits and pieces of you (your energy) were scattered throughout the universe. This has been making you feel less organized, less confident, more spacey, less present, and many other negative things. When the pieces of you are scattered throughout the universe, it's very hard to be in the zone, accessing your awesomeness, loving yourself, enjoying those around you, liking your work, and so on.

So what you are going to do, once you close your eyes to begin the technique, is rewind the explosion. That's right: think of yourself as a Star Wars–type spaceship that was hit by enemy fire, and rewind it just as if you hit the rewind button on the movie. This is exactly what you're going to do by using your imagination, just like a little kid would—without judgment, without worrying whether or not you're doing it right. Just go for it.

In your mind's eye, watch each piece of your energy (or each part of your spaceship) as it careens back through space toward you and then gently lands within you, in exactly the right spot. Imagine that some pieces are coming back to you very quickly and directly with speed and force until they quietly land, while other pieces take longer—perhaps they spin or twirl before they remember their rightful home within your energy body. Remember to imagine the pieces of your energy coming back from behind you, above you, down by your feet, etc. If your energy is scattered, it's not just scattered in one area; it's scatted throughout your body.

As you continue imagining each piece zooming back to your center, notice that you're feeling stronger, fuller, and more badass. Yes, I'm using the word badass! But this is an accurate assessment of what many people have told me they start to feel as their energy returns to them. A lot of people equate badassness with feeling whole and complete, as there is a certain amount of inner power within that starts to become apparent. Wait until you feel that all the pieces that are going to come back to you in this moment have returned, and then sit for a moment feeling this before opening your eyes to experience the difference in feeling, emotion, and energy. In the past, people have told me they felt taller, bigger, longer, fuller, and more solid. They've said that they felt like their eyes were suddenly more open and clear and that they were less tired and happier, even!

Do you see how doing this little exercise that works on your energy also shifted your emotions? Your energy and your emotions are so intimately connected, and that's the beauty of this system. When we shift one, we shift the other. And, boy, is this going to come in handy in this work! Imagine that you're working with your animal, but your energy is chaotic and scattered. It would be hard to notice any messages from your animal when you're feeling dizzy, chaotic, unsure, and more.

When you're first learning the Star Wars Rewind Tool, it will take you about four minutes to complete it, but as you get better and better at it, that time will decrease. At this point in my life, when I've been doing this for more than fifteen years, the exercise takes me about ten seconds. I use it when I feel funky or off and before I meet with any client as well.

Additionally, as you're working with this exercise, it's also important that you set realistic expectations. Don't expect that you're going to pull every single bit of your energy back from every single place it's scattered. We're all human, and we all have things going on in our lives that affect us—and so there is no way you're ever going to achieve 100 percent completely re-formed energy. I've never achieved that, and I don't know anyone who has. Instead, just go by the feel. When you feel you've accepted as much of your energy back as you're going to get in this session, simply allow things to wind down, and sit and experience the positive effects of what you just did. Remember to sit for a minute or two to really enjoy the fruits of your labor before returning to your regular day. Even though it only takes me ten seconds to call my energy back, I always give myself time to feel the shift I just created. I notice what my emotions are; I notice whether I feel fuller or more whole or stronger. Sometimes I may go too fast or become distracted while I'm using the tool, and it's the checking at the end that shows me. If I didn't shift how I was feeling through the tool, I know I need to go back and do it again or try another tool.

So this is really all that energy management is. It's the simple idea of noticing when you are feeling wonky, weird, off, emotional, worried, overstimulated, or anything else that may not make it easy for you to be in the zone, and then it's taking a step (in this case, using the Star Wars Rewind Tool) to shift yourself into a better state of being both emotionally and energetically. The nice part about this type of work is that it doesn't require huge chunks of time. In the beginning it may be four minutes at a time, but as you get better and better, you're probably looking at a minute to do the tool and a minute to feel your accomplishments. This means that tools like this become accessible at almost any time. You can easily grab two minutes during your workday—just by sitting in your cubicle or stopping in your car at a stoplight—to do a little Star Wars Rewind.

Energy management has been made out to be a very time-consuming, big-deal thing. In reality, it isn't.

How to Know When to Do Energy Management

Now that you've learned *what to do* when your energy is off, it would be good to start focusing on *how to know* when your energy is off. I taught you that Star Wars Rewind Tool because I wanted you to experience what it was like to be in the zone. That feeling you had after doing the Star Wars Rewind is the feeling of being in the zone. To know when it would be a good time to use the Star Wars Rewind, you must simply begin noticing when you are not in the zone.

Detecting when you're in and out of the zone can be challenging at first. Like most people, you've probably lived most of your life being mostly out of the zone. Fortunately, once you learn that the zone exists and what it feels like, it can be very easy to develop the awareness necessary to get yourself back into the zone when you've noticed you're out of it. You're already experiencing what out of the zone feels like every day; it's just time to start putting some words and action to it. Here are a few examples that others have come up with for signals that they are out of the zone:

- You start worrying about the end of the world.
- You cry at almost every Facebook post you read about an animal.
- You snap at your partner.
- You worry that your car is unlocked and that someone is going to break in, even though you already checked it.
- You wake up in the middle of the night worried about money.
- You say "I can't" a lot.

- You start comparing yourself to others.
- You find yourself judging everyone who walks by.
- When you drive your car, every other driver around you is an idiot.

These are only a few common examples of being out of the zone. In my private practice, I've had my clients and my students spend a week just taking note of when they are and aren't in the zone. Inevitably, what seems like a momentous task in the beginning (figuring out the signs) becomes very easy within the first few days. Most people start to appreciate patterns in their thoughts or behavior that clearly indicate whenever they are out of the zone, and you will too.

Here's one last thing about energy management. I've taught you the Belly Breathing Technique and the Star Wars Rewind Tool, but there are millions of tools out there that can help you do this. It's important that you find a handful of tools that really work for you so that you can pick and choose what to use in the moment. These tools will not work in every situation—sometimes you're going to need a different tool. This is why it's a good idea to have a few tried and true methods. Especially since, as you develop this new awareness of yourself, you're going to have more and more opportunities to manage your energy!

Remember to have realistic expectations here as well. We are all human. We are all going through our own challenges, learning our own lessons, and experiencing our own lives. This means that at any given time you have at least one thing going on that is going to give you pause, and it will create emotional and energetic shifts. Experiencing emotion is not a bad thing. The goal in energy management is not to remain totally peaceful, calm, and happy all the time. Who can do that? I know I can't, and you shouldn't expect that you can either. The goal is only to notice when you're not in the zone, when an emotion has overridden your balance, and then do what you've now learned to do in order to bring yourself back to the zone. So just give yourself a break, have a good time with it, and start managing, maintaining, and watching. Energy management is not a one-and-done situation. It's an ongoing overseeing of your emotional state that you'll do (and I'll do) again and again for the rest of your life. Eventually, it will be as natural as brushing your teeth.

Case Study: Sandy Smith and Energy Management

I first met Sandy Smith at the Fort Lauderdale airport. As I was standing at the ticket counter checking in for my upcoming flight (I was taking a group of people to Bimini to swim with the wild dolphins), I suddenly heard behind me, "Oh! It's you! I've been following you on Facebook forever! I'm so excited for this trip! It's so funny to see you here! I've been getting your newsletters for years!"

I turned around to see a middle-aged woman with a smile about to burst from her face. Clearly accompanying and supporting her, and carrying most of the bags, was a much more sedate-looking man, Sandy's husband, Rich.

"Hi, Danielle! I'm Sandy! We're coming to Bimini with you to swim with the dolphins! We're so excited! I told my husband he had to come, and so he came and …"

I started to say hello but quickly had to turn back to the desk agent to finish checking in. The woman at the counter politely explained where my next flight would be, how to get there, how much time I had, what to do with my baggage—all that stuff. As I was listening to her, Sandy continued on behind me, "And we have this camera that we just bought and I'm so excited! My husband has snorkeled before, and he ..."

And she kept talking excitedly, happy, and very animatedly.

The station agent had to repeat herself a couple times because I kept turning around to acknowledge my new, very excited student behind me. Once I finished checking in, I told Sandy I would see her at the gate and went on to get breakfast and wait for the rest of the group to arrive. This was my first time taking a group to Bimini, and while I waited, I looked out the window, eating my banana, wondering if everyone was going to be that excited.

I was taking a group of twelve people on this trip, so I knew it would be intimate. That meant, to me at least, that everyone was going to have to learn how to manage their emotions and their energy. No animal wants a dozen overly excited people approaching them with cameras and squeals and splashes and anxiety!

Sandy was, by far, one of the most enthusiastic people I'd ever met. What popped into her head came right out of her mouth! I learned that as she and her husband sat down with the group to share a little bit about themselves. Her husband stayed pretty quiet while Sandy talked up a storm. Her heart was always brimming over with excitement and love but also with anxiety, and I realized that one of the reasons she talked as much as she did was that that was her way of managing her innate sensitivities—it was her work-around.

On our first trip as a group out on the boat to find and then hopefully swim with the wild dolphins, everyone had different emotions. The closer we got to the area where we could possibly see the dolphins, the more talkative (and I realized the more worried) Sandy became. As it turned out, she really wasn't familiar with snorkeling in open water, which was one of the reasons she'd brought her husband along; he turned out to be an expert.

Suddenly the captain slowed the boat and gave us the sign to start donning our gear. As I watched, some people were completely calm and basically jockeying to get in the best position to ascend into that clear turquoise water as soon as possible. Others were slower to get ready, adjusting this, fixing that, forgetting this. Sandy's husband was one of the first into the water with Sandy close behind. I was one of the last.

As I slid into the water, I was surprised that it was so warm. My snorkel, tight on my head, allowed me to take my first look under to ensure that no sharks were coming to get me (yes, that was my main fear), but all I could see were human legs, clear blue water and then, about thirty feet below, gorgeous white sand. As I paddled around, my fins giving me a feeling of superhuman power, the waves around me were pretty choppy. If I stuck my head and snorkel up out of the water, it became a lot of work to find everyone, see the dolphins, and stay up with the boat. I slowly realized that if I stayed in snorkel mode it was easier to be a part of the group.

Sandy, however, hadn't realized this. Within a few minutes of being in the water, she indicated to the captain that she was in trouble. She felt like she was drowning. I could see her panicking in the water, and her husband was swimming in closer to help her. Her little head kept popping up—I could see it in between the choppy waves—and her snorkel and mask were no longer on her face but resting on top of her head. As she and her husband made their way back to the boat (which was twenty or so feet away), I could practically *feel* Sandy's panic in my own body. She glanced over at me as she was hoisting herself onto the boat and I saw the whites of her eyes—she looked petrified.

The dolphins finished their play with the rest of the group a few minutes later and we all pushed through the rough waters to the back of the boat. In all, we'd had about fifteen minutes to play during that session with the dolphins, but when dolphins are done, they're done. That group had moved on. Most of our group de-finned and made their way precariously to the front of the boat to start the search for another group of dolphins while Sandy went below deck with her husband who had his hand gently on her knee as she sobbed and hiccupped for air.

"It wasn't working! I felt like I was dying! I couldn't breathe!" cried Sandy. Her terror and disappointment were apparent in her watery eyes, "I was going to drown! I thought I was going to drown, Danielle!"

I thought for a moment about how to handle this situation. Having already spent a day and a half with Sandy, I knew how emotional and truly sensitive she was. It wasn't just that everything in Sandy's life tended to be dramatic; it was that she felt so deeply everything that she experienced. What someone else might call a slight she would experience as an outright jab. The hardest part about this is that Sandy was not a weak person—it was only that Sandy, being a very sensitive person, had not yet learned how to turn her incredible sensitivity into her power. At this point, her sensitivity was taking her down and making it hard for her to experience life!

I knew what I had to do.

I told Sandy's husband that it was wonderful that he wanted to comfort Sandy, but in order to get herself together so she could go back out in that water, Sandy was going to have to comfort herself. After a moment, he looked at me like I was crazy, gave Sandy a parting hug, and left for the party at the front of the boat.

At first, Sandy wanted to keep talking about how she had almost died in the water. (She hadn't, but I totally understood the feelings she was having.) She kept rehashing her experience with the waves, the snorkel not fitting properly, and not knowing what do to. Finally, I stopped her from talking and calmly explained my thoughts about what was really going on with her, as she sat quietly and dried her tears. I wanted her to understand how sensitive she really was and how, through that sensitivity, she was being overwhelmed by the energy of the waves, the dolphins, the swimming, the people, the snorkel, the fear and more—but she didn't have to be overwhelmed by it. I quickly taught her a breathing technique that she could use right then and there.

As Sandy emerged from the boat's cabin having just completed a few rounds of her new breathing technique, I noticed that her eyes appeared calmer, more relaxed. Instead of darting around, they held my gaze easily, and she smiled.

From that moment on, all I had to do was remind Sandy to do her energy management, and she would find the power within to calm herself, organize her thoughts, ease up on taking things so personally—and connect with the dolphins. We had six more days of that trip together, and not once did Sandy fear she was going to drown again. It was an amazing transformation to watch someone go from feeling and experiencing their world as out of their control to realizing that they had total and complete control, all through energy management.

Sandy has taken several of my classes since this trip, and she is a delight to work with and to be around. Yes, sometimes her energy management flies out the window (oh, you should see her get excited in one of my live webinar classes), but she's since developed the tools and the confidence to bring herself back to center (on her own!), back to that place within her that feels good, positive, and peaceful. Sandy could have chosen to learn the techniques I was teaching her and not incorporate them into her everyday life. Had she done that, she would not be where she is today (and I wouldn't be so excited about having her in my classes). Recently, Sandy was participating in one of my live-stream webinars, and I called on her so she could ask a question. She wanted to give another person in the webinar advice about their own energy management. She said, "I've really got this down now! You might not believe it, but there was a time when Danielle practically ran away from me at the airport!"

Now, I don't remember running away from her at the airport, but I will say that is entirely possible. I can now confidently say that I would *not* consider running away from Sandy if I met her at the airport today.

Chapter Nine

HOW TO COMMUNICATE BETTER WITH ANIMALS

Now that you've learned how to work at the deepest level with your animal, you may be looking for a few shortcuts in the work. I mean, doesn't everyone like to take an easier path? One of those shortcuts is putting yourself in a position to be able to align more completely with the animal in your life. It's all about communication, and I'm not talking psychic communication, although that is certainly a great way to deepen a relationship. Here, I'm talking about taking actions to create the best possible two-way understanding between beings (human and animal).

Some of the most common questions I'm asked are these:

- How can I communicate more clearly or more effectively with my cat/dog/hamster/goat?
- What's the best way to make sure my animal will understand what I want her to know?
- Does my animal really get what I need?

So far, we've spent a lot of time talking about how *you* can understand and most benefit from the message your animal is giving you, but we haven't talked much about things the other way around. After all, in any relationship, we want to be sure that there is a balanced give-and-receive, and as you work to grow your own soul, wouldn't it be great to feel confident that your desires are getting through?

First, the stance that you've had to adopt so far through this book still applies here: animals are incredibly smart, expansive beings that know more than we often give them credit for and often know more than us. Communicating effectively with your pet or that goat on your farm or the rescued llama you met on that trek in Peru won't work if you assume that the animal in question isn't as smart as you are. He simply is. And often, he's smarter because animals always understand the big picture.

Match What You Say to What You Think

As people, what we say often doesn't match what we do. I've had plenty of disagreements with my husband over the years because he has told me that couples time is important to him, but his actions (dedicating his after-work hours to playing hockey, coaching hockey, and working out, for example) told me differently. Animals are the same way. Telling your dog he's the most important being in your life and then failing to take him out and give him enough socialization and walks, for example, tells a very different story to someone who can understand the nuances of life. In fact, in a situation like that, you may end up experiencing a "problem" with that dog because he wants to help you learn how to be reliable and loyal to yourselves and to others (and then you should just reread this book on that one!).

Additionally, the words you use with an animal must not only match your actions but also the visual in your head in order to most clearly communicate your meaning. What do you immediately picture in your mind when you hear the following sentence?

"Get off the sofa!"

Think for a moment.

Now, what did you imagine? You imagined a dog or cat or whoever it was *on* the sofa. Animals are inherently in tune with more than our words; they also pay attention to the tone of our voice, the emotions behind what we're saying, and yes, the images in our head. In fact, many animals communicate in this intuitive way with each other every day! As a regular ol' human, when someone says, "Get off the sofa!" in an angry tone, we're trained to pay attention to two factors: the words that are spoken and the tone in which those words are said. Animals tune in differently. They hear the words we speak, feel the tone in which we say it, and connect to the emotions we're holding, but they also intuitively clue in to the image we hold in our heads. Tuning in this way is a natural part of an animal's ability to survive. So when you angrily say, "Get off the sofa!" while also picturing the animal on the sofa, you are actually sending a mixed message to the animal. You're not being clear in your communication.

Luckily, it's very easy to clean up this aspect of communication with animals. Ensure that you are always present with your animal. This doesn't mean you must spend every minute of every day with him—it only means that when you're hanging out together or spending time around one another, you're completely aware of everything going on with the two of you. Talking on the phone, half-watching TV, chatting with a friend … these are all times when messages can be easily unclear because you are not concentrating on the exact message that you are sending out.

Additionally, changing up how you talk with the animal in your life will help too. Instead of telling your animal to get off the sofa, say, "Go lie down" or "Come sit in my lap." Concentrating on the positive aspects of what you do want rather than concentrating on the behavior that you don't want will work better for you and for the animal in your life. Remember, though, you have to keep your friends and family in line as well. Help them understand how an animal works, and you'll find that everyone's relationship improves.

Match What You Feel to What You Say

As you were going through this book, did you hit a point when you thought, "Well, I'll just pretend I'm not anxious/worried/angry/fearful/insecure/etc., and then all this drama with this animal can be over with!" This seems like a pretty good idea, doesn't it? This animal is helping you learn to believe in yourself, feel powerful, or find peace, so to speed up the process (or perhaps just to get away from the process), pretending that you feel different from how you really feel will sometimes look like a promising option.

It's not.

Remember how I explained earlier about how animals are so in tune with us? Well, this means they are going to figure out you're trying to pull the wool over their eyes. Not only can animals tap into the visuals you carry around in your head, they can also feel the emotions you feel. Animals can naturally sense and experience exactly what we're feeling in very much the same way that you can get off the phone with a friend who's going through a horrible breakup and feel that sadness and anger yourself. Yes, they feel this even when we don't want them to.

As humans, we're used to "putting on a happy face" for our boss; pretending we like a birthday present when inside our head we're saying, "Really?"; or telling ourselves our feelings aren't hurt at our friend's comment when the reality is we're very hurt. People spend a lot of time censoring and adjusting their feelings, thoughts, and emotions to be more politically correct, to be more socially acceptable, to cover up their insecurities, and more. As humans watching all this go down with others, we're really taught to try and take people at face value. If a man is pretending everything is okay, even though you sense something might be amiss, it's not polite to really dig in there and push to get to the crux of the issue. With animals, things are very different.

Animals are not taught to hide their emotions, fears, or thoughts. When an elephant is alarmed, she lets the rest of the herd know it through her trunk. When a cat feels insecure, he takes steps to hide behind the sofa to alleviate those fears. When a dog has anxiety, she shakes. Clear communication among animals has helped them survive and grow for millions of years, and yet on this humans often miss the point—they hide their real feelings from those around them.

It is very disconcerting to an animal when a person feels one way but pretends to feel another way, and many animals will feel this disconnection within and react to it. If you're someone who had the plan to just "pretend" you weren't still feeling a certain way about yourself or believing specific negative things about yourself, you're probably laughing now because you already experienced how badly that backfired. The animal in your life knew exactly what you were doing and upped the game, didn't he?

It's perfectly fine to not always be happy, calm, curious, passionate, or loving around the animal in your life. No animal expects for any person to be in that state all the time. To have the best relationship with your animal, to have the most success in this human-animal relationship work, to be the clearest with your animal, all you have to do is be transparent in who you are, how you feel, and what you're thinking. You know your animal is not going to judge you anyway! So let loose. Be in a bad mood—it's okay. Just remember that the animal in your life is going to do everything in her power to help you shift out of that. And that's not really a bad thing though, is it?

Animals have an inherent ability to forgive. Humans do not. This morning I was looking through my Facebook newsfeed and I came across an informative little photo meme. It was two pictures. The top picture was a barren landscape with the words "A world without bees," and the bottom picture was a photo of a gorgeous jungle with a zebra, parrot, tiger, and more peeking out through vegetation, highlighted by a rainbow. The title of that photo was "A world without humans." This struck me. Not because I didn't believe bees were that important. I certainly believe that. It was more striking that the world can get along so harmoniously without us.

Yes, animals eat animals. Yes, floods and storms occur. Yes, there are challenges. But the animals are so resilient in a way that we humans are not. Unless molested by humans, most animals recover from their traumatic experiences very quickly. They don't sit around worrying, "Will it happen again?" or "What did I do to deserve that?" or "I'm so mad that happened that I'm going to take it out on everyone around me!" In a very survivalist, natural way, animals forgive easily and completely. They view each and every experience as something to learn from—how to be a better stream fisher, how to avoid the tiger next time, how to get that honey more easily. People, on the other hand, hold on to all of that and continually beat themselves up about it.

Be in the Present Moment

The next way to communicate your message to the animal in your life most effectively is to stop making your decisions on how to communicate, what to do, what to say, and how to be, based on how bad you feel for something you did in the past. Animals aren't hooked into the past—they connect in the present moment, and that's all they're looking for from you. Last night, for example, my son, Cole, forgot to walk our dog, Tuukka. Unfortunately, because of the all-day rain we'd been experiencing, that meant that Tuukka was really short-changed on walks.

Now, Cole could have felt terrible for this, fretted over being a bad dog owner, and promised to make it up tenfold the next day, but luckily he's a teenager and didn't do this. Instead, he simply told me (and Tuukka) he would take her for a little longer walk tomorrow. And this is what he did. Without guilt. Without beating himself up, and without worrying about whether or not yesterday's mistake made him a bad person. The result? He and Tuukka had a great walk that was a little longer than usual. Tuukka benefitted from Cole's upbeat demeanor this morning and got a little more excitement and heart in her walk. The connection between them was clear. When you add in guilt, fear, worry, self-criticism, the message becomes marred and stops making sense. Here, the message was clear.

To connect and communicate most effectively with the animals in your life, it really takes being aware of what you're experiencing in the moment and managing that. Animals want us to be clear, happy, concise, transparent, consistent, and powerful in our communication, but when we can't, simply acknowledging this rather than wishing it away or trying to sidestep it will be your next best option. When you consider that the animal in your life understands you, often better than you have understood yourself, it paves the way to letting go of pretense and just going for it. That's what they are looking for anyway!

Don't Expect an Animal to Do the Work for You

Another way to have clear communication with the animal in your life is to be very aware of exactly what you're communicating. In my line of work, I meet people at various stages of challenge in their lives, and often the solution to those challenges is to lean not on a human support system but on the animal. Many people don't want others to know of their pain, their sadness, their grief, or whatever the negative emotion is so they decide to hide their pain from the world, only letting it out when they're in the privacy of their own home with their animal.

What does this look like? It looks like crying every night over your loneliness with your cat in your lap. It looks like allowing yourself to feel your grief but only when your dog is with you. It looks like going through your day in full-blown anxiety but showing it to your bird and no one else. This is a defense mechanism that a lot of people develop when they don't trust people to come through for them or when they don't want anyone to see their own imperfections. It seems like a perfect solution, but it really isn't.

Animals can handle and hold space for a lot of our emotions. After all, you've seen how your cat comes to be with you when you're feeling sad. It's so comforting to have your animal come to your bed, nuzzle your hand, and "be there" for you as you go through your tough time! Animals of all types are willing to do this, but as people we often become dependent on it. This can be a problem because animals aren't just holding space for our emotions—they are absorbing them in exactly the same way that we absorb them. Remember the example earlier about how you can feel upset after being on the phone with an upset person? This is because there is a part of you, and of all people, that can take on the emotions and energy of others. Animals do this same thing.

To have a great, balanced relationship that carries clear communication with your animal, you must manage your emotions yourself. Leaning on your cat or horse for emotional support isn't really fair to the animal who is in your life to help you learn something, not to do the work for you. Why are you leaning on your dog in this way? Why aren't you looking toward your support group instead? And if you don't have a support group, this is something to look at as well!

Just because animals have the capacity to take on our emotions, thereby helping us feel better, it doesn't mean we should take advantage of this. Most likely, if you're finding yourself in a situation like this, you'll be better off going through the human-animal relationship process, so you can change it rather than continuing to rely on your animal in this way. In a healthy, clear relationship with an animal, you have your support system, and you're comfortable relying on it—and any support that your animal gives you is purely a bonus. That way your animal is not taking on your stuff!

Animals of all types—pet and wild—are truly incredible beings, willing to do whatever they possibly can to assist us in alleviating our pain, learning to be our best selves, and creating happiness and unconditional love in our lives. Doesn't it make sense that your interactions, expectations, and experiences with them should be as clear, concise, and full of love as possible?

Animals in Action: Nicole and the Bird in the Purse

When Nicole was a little girl, she felt very lonely. She didn't play often with the other kids on the street, as they tended to be unruly bullies. One day, after returning from school, where she was in second grade, she had time to go out into her backyard and explore. Nicole loved the trees and the grass and always felt happier and less alone when she was able to spend time outside.

While she was flying through the air on her swing, a movement on the ground in her peripheral vision caught her attention. She landed a huge jump off the swing and ran over to check out whatever it was that was squirming around on the ground. It turned out to be a tiny baby bird that had clearly fallen out of the nest from the tree above her.

Nicole ran to get her mother, who wiped her hands on her jean-clad thighs as she came out of the house and said, "It's probably sick, Nicole! Don't touch it!" But it was too late. Nicole had already run ahead and was backtracking with the little guy gently cupped in her hands.

"Mom! We have to save him! He's a baby!" exclaimed Nicole, and Nicole's mom heaved a sigh of giving in.

"Okay, Nicole. Bring him in the house, and we'll make a little nest for him."

For the next week, Nicole and her mom took care of that little baby bird, feeding him mashed up dog food every few hours. Nicole would even wake during the night to reach over and peek into the shoebox to see how he was doing. Finally, Nicole's mom decided it was time to send him back to the wild backyard, as he seemed strong enough to hop around. Like her mom said, "We can't train a bird to fly!"

That day, before Nicole left for school, she and her mom returned the baby to the backyard looking much healthier and happier. They released him in the exact spot where Nicole had originally found him, hoping that his mom would fly down and return him to the nest. Nicole spent that whole day in class feeling proud of herself for helping this baby bird and knew that she wanted to help more animals in her life somehow.

When Nicole returned from school that day, she saw the kids from the neighborhood standing in a pack. They looked excited, and Joshua, the leader, was telling them all to shush. As it turned out, they had caught her baby bird and were walking up and down the street with him in one of the neighbor girl's purses.

When Nicole found out what was going on, she was immediately devastated. Her little guy—the one she'd spent the past week nursing back to help—was trapped by the bullies on the street! She ran inside the house to ask her mom or dad for help, only to realize neither was home, and Mrs. Perkins, who lived in the apartment below, was watching her.

Well, Mrs. Perkins was an old, crotchety woman who only barely watched over her and certainly wasn't about to help her stand up to those bully kids to rescue some bird.

Nicole thought about it. What should she do? Should she wait until her mom returned home from work? It's possible that her baby bird could die before then.

Should she try to distract the kids so that they would drop the purse and start playing with something else? She couldn't think of anything that would be better to play with than a baby bird—and besides, they were bullies. They weren't going to care about anything the lonely girl in the upstairs apartment who never talked to them had to say.

When she saw Joshua throw the bird-filled purse up in the air and then catch it, she realized she had to do something.

Taking a big breath, she put on her biggest big-girl voice and forced herself to march over to the group.

"Joshua! That is *my* bird. I nursed him back to health. You took him from my backyard!" she screamed.

Joshua was startled. What was the quiet girl who never said anything yelling at him for?

Nicole continued. She told him that she would tell everyone at school what he had done and that she was going to have her father come over to their house and talk to him. He was in big trouble. Nicole tried everything she could think of to get her hands on that purse.

And she did. As soon as Joshua handed over the purse, Nicole ran back to her yard and released the little bird, which luckily seemed no worse for wear.

Nicole stayed outside with her bird friend for the next couple of hours, talking with him and petting him until her mom came home. While she sat with him, she realized that what she just did to those bullies—and especially to Joshua—was actually really cool. She'd finally stood up for herself. Well, really she'd stood up for that little bird, but she never would have known that she could do that if she hadn't been so attached to the little guy.

The bird ended up dying, and whether it was from the experience with the neighborhood bullies or because the care that Nicole had given him wasn't enough, it was then that Nicole decided that there was nothing more she wanted to do with her life than help, save, rescue, and fix animals. She knew that it would take quite a voice to do what she wanted to do, but even as a little second grader, she knew that she could do it. Why? Because her experience standing up to those bullies on behalf of her little bird told her so. Before that day, she thought she was destined to be friendless because of how scary Joshua and his friends seemed. That day, her belief began to change, thanks to a little baby bird.

Appendix

COMMON
ANIMAL LESSONS

Over the years that I've been doing this work, I've had the opportunity to learn about the individual animals that are helping the individual people, and this is where we've focused throughout this book. But there is another aspect to this work that we haven't yet acknowledged: in addition to individual animals assisting single or multiple humans, each animal species as a whole is also assisting human consciousness!

Each species embodies a common theme in how animals look to grab the attention of human so that they can start working consciously on their evolution. Here, I've laid out a few of those common themes, but please know that just because a behavior *commonly* means you're working on a particular lesson, it doesn't *always* means you're working on a particular lesson. If you find, however, that you keep pulling up the same general lesson no matter what animal comes into your life, you can bet that you're being given a direction!

If an animal that you're wondering about isn't listed here, you can still figure out what that animal is teaching you; you'll just have to do it manually. Ask yourself what that animal means to you. What does that animal represent? How does that animal live? What characteristic stands out most to you about that animal? You may even choose to look up characteristics about that animal on the Internet.

Dogs, for example, thrive in the human world when they are attached to a human who protects them and has clear boundaries and rules. Many people who have dogs are learning how to step up and be that leader in their life without crossing over into becoming a forceful or aggressive leader. Yes, it's that simple!

Don't worry about what others say that animal is helping you learn—the most important discovery will come through you.

Alligator

Negative Belief: I should put others before myself. My needs are less important than the needs of others.

Embodiment: Alligators are all about territory, and they teach people to hold strong boundaries to protect themselves.

Lesson: It's okay to say no. I deserve to say no. I deserve to keep what is mine.

Antelope

Negative Belief: I can't think on my feet. I can't handle change well. I don't like change that happens fast.

Embodiment: Antelopes help us learn that being quick on our feet does not have to mean losing our balance within, whether that balance is emotional, mental, or energetic.

Lesson: I can be smart and clear. I can be clever and balanced. I can be successful without sacrificing my integrity.

Ape

Negative Belief: I have to do whatever I can to succeed, even if it means disregarding my integrity, not believing in myself, or losing my inner balance.

Embodiment: Apes survive through their integrity, their heart link to their family, and their intelligence. Survival of the fittest incorporates all these qualities.

Lesson: I do not have to sacrifice myself, others, or my integrity to be successful and the best person I can be.

Armadillo

Negative Belief: I don't feel safe, supported, or protected.

Embodiment: Armadillos teach us about innate protection. They don't worry about what is out to get them; instead, they move through their lives knowing they are totally and completely safe and protected.

Lesson: I am safe, supported, and protected by the universe and at the deepest levels possible.

Bacterium

Negative Belief: I must take care of others first.

Embodiment: Bacteria represent balance. Bacteria are not bad or negative, and, in fact, they exist everywhere within life. When they are in balance, things function well. When their numbers are out of balance, life will become clunky, negative, and off.

Lesson: I deserve to put myself first. I deserve to take care of myself. I love balance and can create it by loving myself and giving myself great self-care.

Badger

Negative Belief: I must remain invisible. It's not safe to be noticed. I should try to be like everyone else.

Embodiment: Badgers don't enjoy restrictions, and they'll do whatever they can to break through them—without guilt, anger, or fear. They simply do what they must to live the life they want to live.

Lesson: I can march to the beat of my own drummer with love, honor, and respect. I do not have to rebel—I can just be me.

Bat

Negative Belief: I need to be rescued. I can't handle my life by myself. I need protection from outside of myself. I'm not good enough.

Embodiment: Bats have the ability to sense what others miss. They trust their instinct and inner guidance to provide them with everything they need to live a safe life.

Lesson: I trust myself. I believe in my abilities. I am safe, supported, and protected by myself and by the universe.

Bear

Negative Belief: I need to be one of the majority. I should be like everyone else. I need to travel under the radar.

Embodiment: Bears model being strong and peaceful, aggressive while lazy, and forceful and complacent. True power comes from accepting yourself, even if that self doesn't quite make sense. Bears model this perfectly because it is challenging to apply only one label to them.

Lesson: I am who I am, and who I am is love, awesome, powerful, peaceful, strong, dominant, and clear.

Beaver

Negative Belief: I'm not creative. I'm not good enough. I give up when life gets tough. I don't have the power to complete my goals.

Embodiment: Beavers often take on projects that seem to be impossible (a beaver built a damn here?), and yet they create unwaveringly.

Lesson: My creativity allows me to be successful. I know that I can create whatever I want. I believe in my power to create and succeed.

Bird

Negative Belief: I must force things to happen. Nothing will happen unless I, at all costs, make it happen. I cannot depend on others, only myself.

Embodiment: Inner power comes through flow, through light rather than through heaviness or force.

Lesson: I'm in the flow. My light creates my world.

Bison

Negative Belief: I am a failure. I am weak. I can't do things myself.

Embodiment: Buffalo are strong—whether they are solo or part of the herd, they model physical and mental power.

Lesson: I am strong, powerful, and capable of achieving whatever I set my mind to.

Bobcat

Negative Belief: I'm not safe, supported, or protected. The faster it happens, the better I feel. I don't trust others to get things done, so I'll do it all myself—now.

Embodiment: People who struggle with patience are really struggling to feel safe in the world. Bobcats teach us to trust that the universe will take care of us through their patience and superior hunting skills. They don't worry whether or not they can hunt. They don't worry if their environment will feed them—they trust and attempt, and this allows them great patience and success.

Lesson: I trust that I am safe, supported, and protected. I am patient because I know I am completely taken care of.

Buffalo

See Bison.

Camel

Negative Belief: I am weak. I need rescue. I can't do it myself. I can't make it. I'm not good enough.

Embodiment: Camels demonstrate digging deep within to persevere. Camels rely fully and completely on their own reserves, trusting that they have everything they need to move forward.

Lesson: I can do it. I have exactly what I need to get through anything and everything that is presented to me.

Caribou

Negative Belief: I'm less than everyone else. I need to prove I am the best. I must earn my worth.

Embodiment: Caribou have a simple majesty to them. It's impossible to view a caribou in her natural habitat and not feel her royalty. Caribou model this for us, allowing us to embody our innate beauty and power—and feel free to let others experience this—without dumbing ourselves down.

Lesson: I am powerful. I am beautiful. I am. I allow this to be seen by others.

Cat

Negative Belief: I need the love and approval of others to make me feel good. I need rescue. I need someone else in my life to make me feel whole.

Embodiment: Cats embody independence. They decide when they want affection and when they don't. They call the shots in their life with confidence.

Lesson: I am capable. I am awesome. I do things beautifully on my own.

Cheetah

Negative Belief: I don't trust myself to decide. I always make bad decisions. I need more and more and more information before I can properly figure it out. I need someone to help me, so I can feel safe.

Embodiment: Cheetahs embody confidence within. They survive in the world by making swift decisions and standing by those decisions, unwaveringly.

Lesson: I trust my gut and the decisions that I make.

Chicken

Negative Belief: I don't want to be noticed. It's not safe to be my own person. I want to fly under the radar.

Embodiment: It's surprising to most people, but chickens embody courage to do what you want to do and courage to be who you are, no matter how different that may be.

Lesson: I am strong. It is safe to do my own thing. I trust in my community.

Chimpanzee

See Ape.

Chipmunk

Negative Belief: I can't make it. I'm not strong enough to get through. I'm tired. I'm always out of balance. I don't manage my energy well. I'm always ungrounded.

Embodiment: Chipmunks appear to have an endless supply of energy. This is not because they have superpowers but instead because they know exactly what their body, mind, and energy need, and they work to keep this in balance at all times.

Lesson: I value my body, mind, and spirit, and I take the time to care for myself every day. I put my emotional and energetic needs first, with a deep knowing that this will allow me to be my best self.

Cougar

Negative Belief: I need more data points to figure out the solution. I don't trust my intuition. Logic is the only answer.

Embodiment: Cougars use their incredible observational skills combined with their gut instinct to survive in their world. They model a balance between the logical and the intuitive.

Lesson: I value and work with my logical analysis of my situation and with my intuition surrounding it.

Cow

Negative Belief: I'm not worthy. I'm not deserving. I need to prove I am worthy. I need to earn love and compassion. I'm not lovable.

Embodiment: Cows model living a life in which they must produce to prove their value. All beings deserve life, love, compassion, and family.

Lesson: I am valuable. I am valued. I am deserving regardless of my accomplishments.

Coyote

Negative Belief: I can't figure things out on my own. I always need help. I don't trust that I'll find the best answer myself.

Embodiment: Coyotes are smart and clever and often take unexpected routes to their success. They do this with stealth but also enjoyment. They live their lives joyfully.

Lesson: I am awesome. I am enjoying my life.

Crocodile

See Alligator.

Deer

Negative Belief: I don't trust myself. I'm not sure I can make it happen. I don't believe others will come through for me.

Embodiment: Deer demonstrate the highest trust in their instincts and the instincts of their community. Every day they bet their lives on these things.

Lesson: I am supported. I am safe. I trust my instincts and the instincts of those around me.

Dog

Negative Belief: My life is always out of my control. I feel chaos all the time.

Embodiment: Dogs thrive when their community and home is in balance. This includes having a balanced, clear leader—whether that leader is human or animal.

Lesson: I am in control of my life. I am a leader in my life. I am strong and protective of myself.

Dolphin

Negative Belief: No pain, no gain. I must work hard to achieve what I want in life. Work is difficult and always unenjoyable. If I'm having a good time, I'm not working hard enough. I'm not loveable.

Embodiment: Dolphins teach us to have fun. They are happiest in their lives when they are free, able to play, and communicate. When their fun is taken away, they suffer.

Lesson: I deserve to have fun in my life, and through this fun, other successes, passions, and loves will effortlessly follow. I am in the flow of fun. I will stop turning down fun and enjoy it for what it is—a valuable part of being human. Fun does not take away from my pursuit of success, peace, happiness, or anything else—it adds to it.

Duck

Negative Belief: I can't show who I really am. I don't want anyone to know what I really think or feel. It isn't safe to show my true colors.

Embodiment: Ducks are interesting animals because you always know exactly what you get with a duck. Their integrity in letting what is happening on the inside show on the outside is extraordinary. Simple honesty. The inside matches the outside.

Lesson: It's safe for me to be who I am, to think how I think, and to let my innermost me show through.

Eagle

Negative Belief: I can't do it. I might fail. I don't believe in myself at the deepest level.

Embodiment: Eagles embody confidence extremely well. They believe in their abilities to seek out and hunt down their prey, and they have a great trust in themselves that they can do what they set out to do.

Lesson: I can do it. I trust that I have everything I need to be able to meet my goals in life—both big and small.

Elephant

Negative Belief: I must survive. I must do whatever I can to get through this and be the best. There are no real consequences—only survival.

Embodiment: Elephants are incredible animals that honor everything in their world. They honor their family, the land, the balance of life with the earth, the balance of life with other animals, and more. They are the epitome of balance, gratitude, and respect when allowed to be within their own existence.

Lesson: When I honor myself as well as the family, people, animals, and earth around me, my happiness within and my ability to give and receive love are in complete balance.

Elk

Negative Belief: My life is out of control. Bad things always happen to me. There is chaos wherever I look.

Embodiment: Elk teach us that we can be the leaders of our life, setting our pace, and that the ability to achieve this is all within us already.

Lesson: I am powerful within. I am awesome. I am an innate leader. I lead compassionately with my gut instinct and intuition.

Ferret

Negative Belief: When I hit a roadblock, I stop.

Embodiment: Ferrets are clever, as everyone knows, but what they are really teaching us is about adaptability. They don't let anything stop them from doing what they want to do and will figure out cool and exciting ways to clear any hurdle.

Lesson: I can overcome any obstacle. I believe I have the mind, body, and intuition to get through and find another way.

Fish

Negative Belief: I can't trust others to come through for me. I must do everything myself.

Embodiment: Fish rely on their community to survive. They trust innately that everyone is doing their very best for the good of the whole.

Lesson: I wholly and fully trust in my community that I'm taken care of, just like we all are.

Fox

Negative Belief: I rely solely on my intuition to make all decisions. I rely solely on what others tell me to do to make my decisions. I like data and analysis, and things must all be calculated before I make a move.

Embodiment: Foxes are sensitive animals that survive based on their connection to the world around them. They integrate their intuition with their experience of their environment to stay on their toes and make quick decisions. They teach us that we must have awareness within as well as awareness of our external world to be truly balanced.

Lesson: I'm aware of my intuitive feelings as well as the world around me, and I integrate these so that I can have the best experience possible. I understand that just concentrating on what I want and ignoring the environment, or vice versa, will not produce the happiness and contentment I seek, and it will not benefit the universe either.

Frog

Negative Belief: I can overcome any challenge. I don't need peace around me to be successful. I don't need balance. I can and will power through anything and everything, no matter what.

Embodiment: Frogs are in tune with their environment, preferring to create soft, serene settings based on where they choose to live and how they behave within those environments.

Lesson: I am in the flow with the world around me.

Gazelle

Negative Belief: I don't have enough. It's not enough. It's never enough.

Embodiment: Gazelles model grace for us by being fluid in all that they do. They teach us to hold gratitude for all that we are and all that we possess within us.

Lesson: I am grateful for who I am. I am grateful for my experiences. I can handle all my experiences gratefully and skillfully.

Gecko

Negative Belief: I avoid change. I can't handle change. I am weak. I'm not strong enough. I'm not good enough.

Embodiment: Geckos have bodies that adapt to change extremely well. From drought to a lack of food, they teach us that we have everything within to handle anything the universe throws at us.

Lesson: I am strong and powerful. My inner power allows me to handle all the challenges coming my way. I love and embrace change.

Giraffe

Negative Belief: I'm ugly. I'm not good enough. I'm not like others. I can't handle change.

Embodiment: It's almost impossible for an adult giraffe to be anything but graceful. Even while handling the toughest challenges, a giraffe remains full of grace and beauty, never losing her cool.

Lesson: I can handle the complications and challenges in my life. I am strong, beautiful, and powerful within, and I will remain so even when managing things that may get ugly. Having challenges does not take away from my grace or make me less perfect. I am lovable no matter what.

Goat

Negative Belief: I'm not good enough.

Embodiment: Goats embody being kind, caring, and considerate of those around them without sacrificing their own well-being.

Lesson: I can give to others while also taking care of myself.

Goose

Negative Belief: I must do everything myself. I don't trust others to come through for me. I don't have intuition. I need to figure things out through logic.

Embodiment: Geese work harmoniously within their flocks, knowing when to take charge and when to fall in with the pack. There is no push-pull here—they model support and being supported.

Lesson: I am fully supported by my environment, my experiences, and those around me.

Groundhog

Negative Belief: I can't take care of myself. I need others to help me. I need rescue.

Embodiment: Groundhogs thrive on their own but continue to protect others of their species. They model living a solitary— yet not lonely—life, feeling their power through their ability to take care of themselves.

Lesson: I am perfectly capable of taking care of myself. I love others but do not need others to survive. I can protect myself, and I will be supported if I am ever in need of protection.

Guinea Pig

Negative Belief: I don't try new things. I'm afraid of the new.

Embodiment: Guinea pigs teach us to be inquisitive. Their natural curiosity and lack of fear of checking out new experiences helps teach us to explore without reserve.

Lesson: I am safe to explore anything and everything that strikes my fancy.

Hamster

Negative Belief: Other people annoy me, so I always stay away from them. I don't trust other people. I don't want other people around me. This is the only thing that makes me feel safe. I'm not lovable.

Embodiment: Some hamsters are very social, while others are loners. This depends on what each hamster prefers in the moment. There is no judgment in this, rather only a desire for the hamster to meet his present needs. Hamsters model for us the belief that it's okay to enjoy our support network one day and move away from it another without guilt. Hamsters take care of their social needs perfectly.

Lesson: I make my own choices, free of pressure from others, knowing that these are truly the best options for my greatest and highest good.

Hippopotamus

Negative Belief: Others are always walking over me. I have a hard time saying no. I avoid conflict to the degree that I end up suffering. I'm not lovable.

Embodiment: Hippos know when to keep to themselves and when to stand up for themselves. This balance comes innately within them and is never questioned. They teach us that sometimes it is appropriate to aggressively defend ourselves without apology.

Lesson: I am strong and capable. When I choose to defend myself, it is because it is truly the right time. I believe in my ability to decide when it is the right time to step forward versus the right time to allow things to take place around me.

Horse

Negative Belief: I have too much to do to create balance in my life. I have too many commitments to be able to do the things I really want to do.

Embodiment: Horses are happiest when free, free of restrictions to do what feels best. They teach us that when we rid ourselves of the things that don't matter and focus only on the present moment, we can feel free as well.

Lesson: I have flow in my life. I am powerful. I don't have to worry about what other people think. I can move freely when I listen to my innermost desires.

Hyena

Negative Belief: People are idiots. No one knows what they are talking about. No one seems educated/attractive/fast/etc., enough for my liking.

Embodiment: Humans often misunderstand hyenas. Hyenas are very clever animals, capable of figuring out interesting and surprising solutions. Instead, people get caught up in their seeming "laughter" and fail to notice their intelligence. Hyenas model the idea that you can't judge a book by its cover, and they teach us to give time and space to our experiences and to those in our lives so that we can truly understand what is going on.

Lesson: I'm open to what is happening around me and I no longer rush to judgment. I enjoy understanding the deeper meaning in my world of experiences.

Insect

Negative Belief: I want it now. I don't want to wait. I have a hard time with patience. If things aren't going fast enough, I'll make them go faster.

Embodiment: Insects live complicated lives that often take skill and, even more importantly, patience. Imagine the ant, studiously carrying his load of food all the way back to his anthill, or the bee, searching miles to find the best flowers to pollinate. Insects model patience. Patience is easy for these insects to achieve because they have an innate belief that their needs are provided for.

Lesson: I am safe, supported, and protected. All my needs are met; therefore, I am patient to allow this to happen. I am in the flow.

Jaguar

Negative Belief: I don't feel comfortable being alone. I need others to make me feel safe. I must do everything on my own because I don't trust others to support me. I must earn the love of my peers.

Embodiment: Jaguars are beautiful, mostly solitary animals that model a balanced independence. They spend most of their lives alone—except during mating season.

Lesson: I am independent, yet when I need something from others, I trust that I can find it.

Jellyfish

Negative Belief: I'm not important. I don't matter. No one cares about my opinion. People don't listen to me. I'm not lovable.

Embodiment: Jellyfish are a significant part of the big picture in the ocean. They eat and are eaten. They serve a great purpose, and without them, the ocean inhabitants could no longer survive. Humans are mostly afraid of jellyfish and fail to recognize their importance, but they model that everyone and everything is an important part of the world.

Lesson: I am worthy. I am important. My existence is a great contribution to the world, even when I may not know what the contribution is. I am lovable.

Kangaroo

Negative Belief: I don't have what I need to feel powerful. I am powerless. I'm always out of balance.

Embodiment: Kangaroos model balance. When you look at the body of the kangaroo, it appears as if there is a lack of balance within this animal (built in a seemingly bottom-heavy way), yet they have learned how to work with their bodies (with what they have) to create power and balance within.

Lesson: I use all the pieces available to me to create balance in my life.

Koala

Negative Belief: I must always be "on" to ensure that things go smoothly. I can never take my eye off the ball.

Embodiment: Koalas are … koalas. And they feel no need to prove their value or worth to anyone, even themselves. They take life at their own pace and do what works for them to feel happy, content, and peaceful and have a full belly, with an innate understanding that what serves them also serves the greater good.

Lesson: I am who I am, and who I am is love, awesome, powerful, peaceful, strong, dominant, and clear. I do not need to prove my value to anyone, even myself. I am perfect in my imperfections.

Lemur

Negative Belief: Everyone else's needs seem to come before mine. I'm always the low man on the totem pole. I need to prove my value so that others will pay more attention to me, support me, and love me.

Embodiment: Lemurs teach us about support. Family is of the highest priority to lemurs, and in their family they each give and receive attention, care, and love. Lemurs don't question their worthiness to receive that love. Instead, they know exactly where they are in their family structure, and their needs and desires match that completely.

Lesson: I deserve support, care, kindness, and love. I am lovable. I am completely supported, protected, and secure within my group structure (family, work, etc.).

Lion

Negative Belief: I must take care of myself at all costs. I must put myself ahead of my friends and family—and that is justified because I have no other choice.

Embodiment: Lions are typically associated with power and strength, but what they are really teaching us about is structure, organization, and honoring what has been put together. A pride of lions has a specific hierarchy, with each lion playing

its own role based on that lion's strengths and weaknesses. It is
the respect of this structure that allows the pride to function
well.

Lesson: I am organized. I understand my role in the world.
I honor the way the world works.

Lizard

Negative Belief: It is not safe to let others know how I really think
or feel. It's best to keep my real feelings inside.

Embodiment: Lizards work with inner power and independence.
Ever vigilant, they are in tune to what is going on around
them, combining this with a strong belief in themselves and
their power in order to survive.

Lesson: I am in tune with my inner self as well as my environment. Both the inside and the outside work in unison to
create and provide flow and balance.

Llama

See Camel.

Lobster

Negative Belief: It's better to be part of the herd. It's safer to fly
under the radar by blending in with my actions, decisions,
and thoughts.

Embodiment: Lobsters scavenge for food and are totally content to
do so. They teach us to feel comfortable creating our life in our
own way, regardless of what others say about our decisions.

Lesson: I don't have to have all the answers at once. I am happy
to piece things together to form my own truth, even when
others would scoff at me.

Loon

Negative Belief: I must analyze everything before making a decision. It's not safe to be spontaneous. If I am unsure, the best answer is to stay put and gather more data—a lot more data.

Embodiment: Loons spend their lives diving deep into the water to find what they need. They don't worry whether the water is cold, and they don't fear they won't like what they find. They simply and powerfully go deep and trust.

Lesson: When I look deeply at myself, I like what I see, and I know that everything that I see is exactly enough. I am wonderful, awesome, and powerful from the inside out.

Monkey

See Ape.

Moose

Negative Belief: I must put pressure on my world to produce what I want. I can never let up on myself, or what I'm trying to achieve won't happen. Push, push, and push. If it doesn't make sense logically, then there is no reason to do it.

Embodiment: Moose teach us the difference between power and force. Moose rely on natural power and intuition, not on intimidation and pressure, to make a life for themselves.

Lesson: My peace and power within allow me to accomplish what I'm here to accomplish. I do not need to push or prove, for I am awesome just the way I am.

Mountain Goat

Negative Belief: I worry about the future all the time. I wake up worrying. My anxiety helps keep me on top of everything and helps me to feel safe.

Embodiment: Mountain goats are kings at going with the flow, being in the present moment, and doing what feels good right now. They don't worry about the future or hang on to the past. Instead they teach us how beautiful life is when we are fully present with it.

Lesson: I am safe, supported, and protected. All my needs are met. I am in the flow.

Mountain Lion

Negative Belief: I will hurt other's feelings if I have boundaries. Other people can't survive when I take care of myself. It is not okay to put my self-care ahead of the care of others.

Embodiment: Mountain lions are all about boundaries—they model how well holding a strong internal boundary works.

Lesson: I can decide what I want. I can do this with love, and, yes, it can benefit me. I am happy to say no when I feel no applies.

Mouse

Negative Belief: I need to be rescued. I need to ask family and friends for advice for each move I make. I don't come up with solutions myself without getting help. I'm needy.

Embodiment: Mice pay attention to everything and then gloriously put it all together to understand exactly what they need to do next. They model being able to look at all the details while also being able to step back and understand the big picture.

Lesson: I am smart, capable, powerful, and fully able to understand my situation. I do not need rescuing. I can figure out both the steps to take and the overall lesson beautifully on my own.

Octopus

Negative Belief: I can't do it. I might fail. It's too hard for me. I'm not smart enough.

Embodiment: The octopus is surprisingly smart and dexterous. He models finding new and unconventional ways to accomplish what we want to accomplish.

Lesson: I can figure out the answer. I am smart.

Opossum

Negative Belief: I like things to go in the direction I want for them to go. I don't like when things change under my feet. I like control.

Embodiment: The opossum is often made fun of in cartoons for playing dead in stressful situations, but it is exactly this that she is teaching us. Opossums are clever and willing to do whatever it takes to move through a challenge. Rather than making fun of that, we can learn from it. When you remove your expectations about what conquering your challenge looks like, you'll be opening yourself to even better solutions.

Lesson: I have released my expectations about what it all has to look like, and I'm happy to go with what the universe is showing me.

Ostrich

Negative Belief: I'm not strong/powerful/balanced/clear enough to handle this.

Embodiment: Ostriches look as if they would have a difficult time maneuvering their bodies; however, their bodies are perfectly balanced between top and bottom, allowing them to quickly address any challenges that come their way.

Lesson: Keeping myself in balance physically, emotionally, mentally, and energetically allows me to be flexible and think on my feet quickly.

Otter

Negative Belief: I shouldn't do what makes me happy because other people won't understand it.

Embodiment: Otters help us align with that which is peaceful for us and only us by embodying this in their everyday life. Most wouldn't enjoy drifting down a cold river on our backs, but otters know this is what works for them and go for it.

Lesson: I deserve to do for myself that which truly makes me happy—even if no one else gets it.

Owl

Negative Belief: I'm not good enough. I'm not smart enough.

Embodiment: Of course owls model intelligence, but they also teach us about allowing. As great hunters, owls aptly determine the best course of action—and often the best course of action is to wait. They trust that their instincts, surroundings, and skills will help them procure exactly what they need.

Lesson: I trust in my ability to figure out any challenge. I am smart, capable, and finely tuned to procure and create for

myself everything that is necessary in this life to feel passionate, happy, sated, and peaceful.

Panda

Negative Belief: I need to be the best I can possibly be. I must
win. I must prove my value. I'm not loveable.

Embodiment: Pandas are not concerned with proving themselves—instead they go about their business with a clarity of
purpose that allows them to feel peace. They teach us that no
pressure is needed to experience peace within, only a following of flow and passion.

Lesson: I am in the flow and follow my passion. Nothing else is
needed within me other than enjoying the ride within, and I
will be completely taken care of.

Panther

See Cougar.

Parrot

Negative Belief: I need others to see how smart I am. I look to
others for validation on my physical looks. I tell people what
they want to hear so they will like me. I'm not lovable, so I
seek approval through others.

Embodiment: Parrots are much wiser than humans typically give
them credit for. They model feeling happy and content with
themselves—despite what others think or say.

Lesson: I don't need to prove my worth or lovability. I like myself
just the way I am, and those who can't see that will be blinded
by my happiness, generosity, and smile one day.

Penguin

Negative Belief: I am lost without a partner. I am only complete with a partner. I am only complete when I have a big group of friends.

Embodiment: Penguins rely on themselves, their chosen mate, and the group in general to live. They consistently balance all these parts of their lives based on the conditions in their life. For example, sometimes they will lean more on their mate (to raise offspring), while other times they will demonstrate their strength (to become one of the dominant penguins). Penguins model achieving balance within ourselves as well as with those around us.

Lesson: I trust myself and others to protect me and support me.

Pig

Negative Belief: I'm always off. There is chaos around me. I feel like my life is out of my control.

Embodiment: Pigs love stability and they thrive when their environment, their support system, their family, and everything else is balanced. They teach us to embrace our own form of balance, even if it doesn't look like what others would call balance.

Lesson: I have the skill to find and maintain my life balance regardless of what others think, feel, or say.

Platypus

Negative Belief: I'm safe when no one notices me. I'm happy to let others take the credit for my work. I like to fly under the radar. I prefer not to speak up.

Embodiment: The platypus models simply being. The platypus believes in herself strongly, regardless of the opinions of those around her. She does not allow herself to be swayed into behaving any way other than her own way.

Lesson: I am who I am, and who I am is awesome. I march happily and freely to the beat of my own drum. I am wonderful. I am lovable. I am worthy, capable, and deserving of my opinions. Others can benefit from what I have to say as well.

Polar Bear

Negative Belief: I'm not strong. I'm weak. I have to watch out, as I can be easily taken advantage of. I don't trust myself or others to care for me.

Embodiment: Polar bears teach us to believe in our abilities to dig deep and keep going, even in times of turmoil. Polar bears intuitively trust in their environment and that they are taken care of.

Lesson: I have what it takes to make it through any challenge. I am strong and powerful, spirited and intuitive. I know that as I dig deep, additional support will show up to help me as well, as I am safe, supported, and protected by the universe.

Porcupine

Negative Belief: I must do everything myself. I don't trust others to come through for me. I'm very independent.

Embodiment: Porcupines are mostly solitary animals, seeking others only in times of need (such as bad weather). They model for us an independence that shifts to working with a group when necessary. They do not cling to their independence, although they do value it.

Lesson: I trust others to come through for me when I ask for their help, but I am happy to take care of myself as well. In doing so, I feel full.

Porpoise

Negative Belief: The goal is all that matters. I need to exceed all my expectations. As I approach a goal, I should up the ante.

Embodiment: Porpoises teach us about enjoying our lives. They represent fun, passion within, and the ultimate, everyday pursuit of that experience.

Lesson: I deserve to have fun in my life, and through this fun other successes, passions, and loves will follow. I am in the flow of fun. I will stop turning down fun and value it for what it is—a respected part of being human. Fun does not take away from my pursuit of success; it is a huge part of it.

Rabbit

Negative Belief: I must protect myself all the time. I must watch out for myself. No one else will watch out for me or come through for me. I'm not lovable.

Embodiment: Rabbits embody living with love every day. Family is the most important aspect to them, and they will do everything they can to promote their family's health and happiness.

Lesson: I am in tune with my family and friends around me. I trust them, and they trust me, as we live and grow together faithfully.

Raccoon

Negative Belief: I don't trust others to come through for me. I don't believe that I am taken care of by anyone. I don't have the resources within me to be or feel successful.

Embodiment: The raccoon is comfortable using all her tools to feed and protect herself and her family. Outside of that, she scavenges for whatever else she needs, fully knowing that the needs will be met. She teaches us to believe in our inner power while also using the advantages our environment offers us.

Lesson: I believe I am strong, capable, and powerful—enough to serve my family in whatever way is necessary. I trust that I am being shown everything I need in life.

Rat

Negative Belief: I can't create my life. I'm a victim of my circumstances. I have no control over my life.

Embodiment: Rats are clever and do whatever they need to do to care for themselves. Often they surprise others with their ability to create homes, find food, and more.

Lesson: I have the intelligence, smarts, and skills needed to create the life I want.

Rhino

Negative Belief: I don't have time to deal with my feelings of anxiety, lack of confidence, or imbalance. I can push through everything anyway.

Embodiment: Rhinos model being grounded, balanced, clear, and powerful. Imagine a rhino running toward you. Feel the power? This is what they show us so that we can create it in our own life. Being fully present and clear produces that inner strength and power.

Lesson: I am aware of my energetic balance and do whatever is necessary to bring myself into balance. My balance and clarity are a great contributor to my power within.

Rooster

Negative Belief: It's better to be part of the herd. It's safer to fly under the radar by blending in with my actions, decisions, and thoughts. It is better to hide.

Embodiment: Roosters march to the beat of their own drum. They represent following one's heart, regardless of the pack.

Lesson: I believe in myself. I believe in my power. I can do my own thing easily and without resistance. I'm not worried about what others think because I know I'm doing what is for my greatest and highest good; therefore, it's for the greatest and highest good of all.

Sea Lion

Negative Belief: No pain, no gain. I must work hard to get what I want. Fun is overrated.

Embodiment: Sea lions teach us to take our lives seriously without ever losing our sense of humor. Sea lions take care of themselves well, and this includes taking downtime.

Lesson: I can work efficiently and still leave time for myself. I deserve time too.

Seal

See Sea Lion.

Seagull

Negative Belief: Nothing ever comes my way. Everything works out for everyone else, but it never happens for me. I never win anything. Everyone else has it easier than I do.

Embodiment: Seagulls model being an opportunist and taking total care of themselves. Ego doesn't get in the way; they do what is good for them to live. They don't worry about whether they deserve that fish or that bit of food—they just know they deserve it.

Lesson: I am deserving and completely supported by my life and environment, which gives me everything I need to live just like everyone else. I can figure out answers to any challenge.

Shark

Negative Belief: I don't have the focus/strength/prowess/skills/ intelligence/power/etc., to reach my goals and be happy.

Embodiment: When sharks decide they want something, they focus in on it and strive to achieve it. They don't question whether they can achieve it, they simply believe in their power (physical and mental) and go for it.

Lesson: I am strong, powerful, and awesome enough to focus in and achieve what I want in my life. I can do it.

Sheep

Negative Belief: It's better to be part of the herd. It's not okay to go against the norm. I should keep my alternative ideas to myself.

Embodiment: Sheep usually appear in great numbers, making it tough to tell one apart from the other, and yet each sheep is powerful in knowing exactly who he or she is.

Lesson: It's okay for me to stand out. I am different, and I love this about myself. I am safe to be myself.

Sloth

Negative Belief: I don't have time to do the things I want to do. I don't have time for myself.

Embodiment: Sloths embody extreme self-care. They do only what feels good: eating, sleeping, climbing, and enjoying the sunlight ... They teach us to take time for ourselves so we can be healthy, happy, content people.

Lesson: I can do the things that make me happy.

Snake

Negative Belief: I am different; therefore, I am less. I am ugly. I am feared.

Embodiment: Snakes, despite being feared by many animals and humans alike, continue to do their thing, live their life, and perform their very valuable functions in the world. They do not bow to pressures.

Lesson: I am free to be me, to march to the beat of my own drum. I don't have to be accepted by everyone, only my inner self.

Spider

Negative Belief: I overgive and sacrifice to make others happy. I hide my feelings to make others happy. I dumb myself down, so others can feel comfortable to be around me.

Embodiment: Spiders know and live with the ultimate balance. They model knowing exactly how much to put out and how much to bring in. Just look at the beauty of their webs.

Lesson: When I honor my intuition and inner knowing, I find balance in giving and receiving.

Squid

Negative Belief: No one understands me.

Embodiment: Squids teach us to take advantage of whatever method works best for us to communicate our ideas. Squids flash and use bursts of color to get their message through because this is how they are best suited. For you, it may be drawing, writing, dancing, speaking, and organizing.

Lesson: I have everything I need to get my message through. I can communicate well, in my own personal way, even if it's not the way that others may typically communicate.

Squirrel

Negative Belief: Well, this is as good as it gets. This is the best that I can have even though it's not really what I was looking for.

Embodiment: Squirrels are not satisfied until they have gathered exactly what they need. They don't settle. They don't say, "Eh … hopefully, this will get me through the winter!" They go after what they want and don't settle. They keep going until they have achieved their goals.

Lesson: I deserve for things in my life to work out the way I would like. I am worthy of having my life feel the way I want it to feel. I deserve a wonderful life, partner, job, and day.

Starfish

Negative Belief: I can't have any less than I have and still be okay.

Embodiment: Starfish teach us about flexibility and adaptability. When a starfish loses one of its arms, the starfish will adapt accordingly, working to regrow that arm.

Lesson: I can adjust and handle any change that comes my way, whether positive or negative.

Swan

Negative Belief: I lose myself in relationships. I forget what my own needs are.

Embodiment: Swans embody balance with another. They form bonds with their partner and work in tandem to achieve a harmonious, balanced relationship.

Lesson: I can have a clear, balanced, intimate relationship in which I take care of myself as well as my partner. This relationship is satisfying because two whole people come together to complement each other.

Tiger

Negative Belief: It's best to be stoic. It's best to keep my feelings and thoughts a secret. This behavior keeps me safe.

Embodiment: Tigers are focused yet intuitive. They maintain an awareness of their surroundings at all times while also being aware of themselves. They represent an inner and outer balance that results in great success.

Lesson: What is on my inside is completely reflected on the outside. I am in tune with my emotions and like them, whatever they are. I feel safe to share my feelings with those around me.

Turkey

Negative Belief: I want more. I should have more. Others have more; why can't I? I want it bigger and better.

Embodiment: Turkeys teach us about being grateful for what we have in front of us. Turkeys are opportunistic feeders—they eat what the world is providing for them rather than turning their nose up, being picky, or refusing. They model gratitude for what they have.

Lesson: I am grateful for the things, people, and experiences in my life, and I know that this gratitude creates more things, people, and experiences to be grateful for.

Turtle

Negative Belief: There are too many obstacles for me to achieve my goals. I can't do it.

Embodiment: Turtles do what they do. When something occurs and they need to stop, they stop, take cover, and then resume doing what they're doing when the danger has passed. They embody simply and peacefully sticking to goals, despite any hiccups or challenges.

Lesson: I can do what I've set out to do. I can achieve my goals, even if it takes me some time.

Vulture

Negative Belief: I don't trust others to come through for me. I don't believe that I am taken care of by anyone. For me, it's all for one—me.

Embodiment: It's probably unexpected, but vultures teach us about loyalty. Vultures are committed to their families and strive to protect them in all situations. This creates a strong support system that the entire vulture family feels secure in relying on.

Lesson: I trust my family and friends to come through for me, and they trust me to do the same. I feel safe and supported by my social network. I feel safe in the world.

Walrus

Negative Belief: Hiding my feelings and thoughts keeps me safe and prevents others from figuring out that I'm not good enough.

Embodiment: Walruses thrive through communication. They model creating their desired life through communion, connection, and communication (grunting, whispering, roaring, coughing).

Lesson: I can communicate my feelings freely and powerfully. My feelings are valid, and I can easily let others know about them. I feel safe to share what is going on within me.

Weasel

See Ferret.

Whale

Negative Belief: It's not worth it to tell others what I think. No one understands me, so why talk? No one listens to me, so why should I listen to them?

Embodiment: Whales model the ultimate in communication. When you observe a pod of whales, you'll not only see that they are in touch with each other physically, but you can also hear it. Whales teach us to value what we have to say to our peers—and what they have to say to us. So many people have underestimated the value of clear communication!

Lesson: I feel comfortable sharing my thoughts and feelings with others. I know that my peers value my words, and I value what they have to say and teach me.

Wolf

Negative Belief: I don't work well with others. I don't like working with others. I don't trust others to come through for me. I'm not lovable, so I'll just take care of it all myself since no one else will.

Embodiment: Wolves teach us about working together as a unit. Whether it's family or the pack, wolves model this for us in their everyday life.

Lesson: I trust others to come through for me. I believe in my support system. I work well within my support system.

Woodchuck

See Groundhog.

Worm

Negative Belief: Why try? I'm nobody anyway. I don't matter. I'm not big/smart/famous/established/successful/etc., enough yet.

Embodiment: Worms may seem somewhat unimportant, but they are actually very important. They take care of the earth just by their movements! They feed many birds and animals as well. Worms embody the idea that no matter how insignificant we may feel, our efforts, our thoughts, and our existence matter greatly.

Lesson: Everything I do affects the rest of the world in some unseen way. I am just as important and worthy as every single other soul, whether human or animal, on this earth.

Zebra

Negative Belief: I don't feel safe being noticed. I want to fly under the radar. Others will target me if I stand out.

Embodiment: Every day zebras model the beauty of standing out, of marching to the beat of our own drum, of being an individual.

Lesson: I feel safe, supported, and protected by the universe being me, even though being me doesn't look like being anyone else.

To Write to the Author

If you wish to contact the author or would like more information about this book, please write to the author in care of Llewellyn Worldwide Ltd. and we will forward your request. Both the author and publisher appreciate hearing from you and learning of your enjoyment of this book and how it has helped you. Llewellyn Worldwide Ltd. cannot guarantee that every letter written to the author can be answered, but all will be forwarded. Please write to:

Danielle MacKinnon
℅ Llewellyn Worldwide
2143 Wooddale Drive
Woodbury, MN 55125-2989
Please enclose a self-addressed stamped envelope for reply,
or $1.00 to cover costs. If outside the U.S.A., enclose
an international postal reply coupon.

To contact Danielle online, visit www.daniellemackinnon .com. For more information, please visit our website at http:// www.llewellyn.com.

Identify, Attune, and Connect to the
Energy of Animals
Animal
Frequency
Melissa Alvarez
A REFERENCE TO 200 WILD, DOMESTIC,
AND MYTHICAL CREATURES

Animal Frequency
Identify, Attune, and Connect to the Energy of Animals
MELISSA ALVAREZ

Discover the energetic power of animals and how to connect with their frequencies in order to grow spiritually. This easy-to-use, A-to-Z reference guide contains encyclopedic listings for nearly two hundred animals—wild, domestic, and mythical—and easy techniques and visualizations for building relationships with them, including energetically bonding with your pets. All animals possess a distinctive energy vibration that can connect with yours, allowing you to communicate with them and understand their role in your spiritual development.

978-0-7387-4928-0, 432 pp., 7 ½ x 9 ¼   **$24.99**

LLEWELLYN'S

COMPLETE BOOK OF

MINDFUL LIVING

AWARENESS AND MEDITATION PRACTICES
FOR LIVING IN THE PRESENT MOMENT

Including Michael Bernard Beckwith, Jack Canfield,
Cyndi Dale, Guy Finley, Rolf Gates, and Thomas Moore

ROBERT BUTERA, PhD and ERIN BYRON, MA

Llewellyn's Complete Book of Mindful Living
Awareness & Meditation Practices
for Living in the Present Moment
ROBERT BUTERA, PHD, AND ERIN BYRON, MA

Enhance your awareness, achieve higher focus and happiness, and improve all levels of your health with the· supportive practices in this guide to mindful living. Featuring over twenty-five leading meditation and mindfulness experts, *Llewellyn's Complete Book of Mindful Living* shows you how to boost your well-being and overcome obstacles.

With an impressive array of topics by visionary teachers and authors, this comprehensive book provides inspiration, discussion, and specific techniques based on the transformative applications of mindfulness: basic understanding and practices, better health, loving your body, reaching your potential, and connecting to subtle energy and spirit. Using meditation, breathwork, and other powerful exercises, you'll bring the many benefits of mindfulness into your everyday life.

978-0-7387-4677-7, 384 pp., 8 x 10 **$27.99**

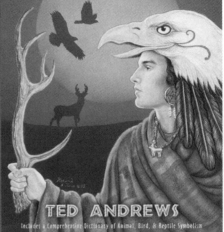

ANIMAL SPEAK

The Spiritual & Magical Powers of Creatures Great & Small

TED ANDREWS

Includes a Comprehensive Dictionary of Animal, Bird, & Reptile Symbolism

Animal Speak
The Spiritual & Magical Powers of Creatures Great and Small
Ted Andrews

Open your heart and mind to the wisdom of the animal world. *Animal Speak* provides techniques for recognizing and interpreting the signs and omens of nature. Meet and work with animals as totems and spirit guides by learning the language of their behaviors within the physical world.

Animal Speak shows you how to identify, meet, and attune to your spirit animals; discover the power and spiritual significance of more than 100 different animals; call upon the protective powers of your animal totem; and create and use five magical animal rites, including shapeshifting and sacred dance.

This beloved, best-selling guide has become a classic reference for anyone wishing to forge a spiritual connection with the majesty and mystery of the animal world.

978-0-87542-028-8, 400 pp., 7 x 10   **$22.99**

To order, call 1-877-NEW-WRLD
Prices subject to change without notice
Order at Llewellyn.com 24 hours a day, 7 days a week!

the BOOK of
DOG
MAGIC

SPELLS, CHARMS & TALES

SOPHIA
with Denny Sargent

The Book of Dog Magic
Spells, Charms & Tales
SOPHIA WITH DENNY SARGENT

Enter the realm of dog magic, where you'll develop incredible relationships with your canine friends that allow you to know what your dogs are thinking, see through their eyes, heal physically and emotionally through your spiritual bond with them, and more. Filled with stories, spells, charms, and exercises, *The Book of Dog Magic* shows you how to understand your pets on a deep, even psychic, level.

Join authors Sophia and Denny Sargent as they explore the history, mythology, and cultural impact of canines. Discover magical techniques to teach obedience, invoke your dog totem, and connect with a dog in the afterlife. You and your furry friends will love this comprehensive, easy-to-use guide.

978-0-7387-4638-8, 264 pp., 5 x 7   **$16.99**